My Collective –

MY
THE DARK SIDE OF ME
PART ONE

In life I see the dangers
The sorrows of humanity
The choices we've made
And as sorrows unfold
Grow in leaps and bounds
The savagery of humanity remains

In the darkness I see the moon
A full moon, crescent moon even a small moon
In the midst of it all I see only pain
Humanity truly gone

BY

MICHELLE JEAN

Before I continue to edit this book I have to do or say this first. By now you'll know that it can take years or month before I edit my books – correct them. Yes I linger too much and I have to stop this because we are all living on free food ticket – borrowed time.

Remember I gave all of you three dates 1313, 2032, 2132 and I said I did not see disaster associated with 2032 because it was way too far in time. Well I can confirm the worst. This is no prediction this is confirmation. The worst has come because there is no extension of time. Humanity will not see 2132.

I do not know what the hell is going on with New York but New York the shit you are going on with behind closed doors have to stop because your city will be destroyed again. I cannot keep seeing destruction coming to you.

There is a war coming brewing and America it will hit your soil because New York will become target practice for the undead – dead. So America think about what you're because the destruction of New York – your land will not be pretty. You are forewarned.

Yes I know what belongs to the devil belongs to the devil and what belongs to God belongs to God but guess what earth cannot sustain any more damage. It can no longer maintain and sustain evil – sin because sin has and have destroyed this planet. We are the ones aiding sinful and wicked people to destroy this world – planet and right now death is knocking and taking and we are not seeing this. Meaning we are ignoring death. Trust me the door of God is just about closed and it is time now for God's people to get on board to God and leave evil – sin to his destruction.

Good can no longer maintain evil on this planet because all that evil is doing is wrong – sinful. Evil is causing this planet as well as you the individual to die.

This is your final warning and if you ignore it then it will truly be too late for humanity and mankind.

Because of the dream I had I had to interrupt the editing of this book because for some reason it went unedited. And in truth too I forgot that I wrote it and yes I am bad at organizing my work because I have so many on the internet that I forget them.

Compared to some people I don't have a lot but when you are doing it yourself it is a lot – extremely hard. Trust me it takes years sometimes.

Like I've told you in my other books women hold the keys to physical time and this is done thru our bloody 28 day cycle. We cannot change this because this is true earthly time – physical time.

Spiritual time has nothing to do with physical time and you should know this because time is in time in another place and time meaning time is in time hence man cannot and will never correlate or decipher true time.

Man does not have the keys to time in time because this key only God has hence God is time in time.

And no, this is not confusing because if you knew time you would know that this time is the real time.

We say there is a time to live and a time to die but there is no time to live. Life cannot die and life moves forward in time to a greater space and time. A time and space that is infinitely more beautiful than the space and time we have on earth.

I repeat Life cannot die. Life moves forward to a greater space and time. One that is infinitely more beautiful than the space and time we have on earth.

This truth infinitely cannot change and infinitely will never ever change so know this because this is knowledge.

Life hath time to live some of you may be saying but this is infinitely incorrect. Life hath no time meaning life is not defined by time or space but death is.

Everything that is in the universe and galaxies hath life and with life everything grows. It cannot stay the same it must grow and it does grow and move forward hence man cannot comprehend the universe or time.

Time was given to death and no one else. I repeat time was given to death and no one else. Death hath time to kill – take evil life. It is only evil life that death takes. Death cannot take good life because good life cannot die. Only evil life dies.

Well my body dies you are saying. Your body is not true life it is just a conduit or conductor for the spirit. The body – flesh is your living soul in your book of sin but sometimes we use the soul to refer to the spirit and this is because the body or flesh houses the spirit. If I am confusing you just look at a dead body whether it be in the movie or at the house of the dead. When you see the dead body it hath no life right?

Yes
Once life meaning the spirit leaves the body the flesh dies go back to the earth – ground and worms eat it but the spirit – that electrical current moves on to greater life if you are good but dies if you are sinful – wicked – evil.

So know that death cannot take true and good life it can only take evil life – what belongs to him.

Remember what belongs to God belongs to God and what belongs to death belongs to death. God who is life cannot interfere with death and his people. Infinitely know this. God cannot interfere with deaths people.

Evil takes what does not belong to him. Yes in the physical sense but evil cannot take what does not belong to him in the spiritual world. This is impossible and infinitely cannot be done.

The reason this is so is because we gave evil access to earth. If we did not do this evil could infinitely never come in hence I will forever tell you the truth of evil. Evil makes his lies seem like the truth and you have to go back to Genesis and read the lie evil told Eve.

We cannot forget that there are two Gods. The God of Life and the God of Death and this is why I ask America in my other book which god do they trust?

Is it the God of Life or the God of Death? No one can have both you can only one hence we have Will.

On resurrection day I will choose and I will choose God on that day.

Infinitely never gonna happen hence I tell you the life in the physical determines where you go in death – the grave.

Resurrection Day is not for those that are good it is for those that are evil. Evil people – spirits are the ones to be judged hence the book of Judges.

There is no way that Good can be judged. No good will be judged if their goodness outweighs their sins. Absolutely no one can judge a good man or woman for their good deeds. This is infinitely impossible.

If God or any judge a person for their good then God himself have to judge himself because he created everything good and out of true love. So infinitely no, good cannot be judged.

Tell me can a man judge God?

Don't even go there because holding God accountable of sin is not the same as judging God. No man can judge God because we do not know how God came into being or created this universe like I've said before.

Death is severe because it is the harshest punishment a spirit can get.

Death is final and absolute. No one can change this.

What about the key of death?

Do not worry about the key of death because this key does not represent the spiritual world it represents the physical world. No this is a poor explanation because there is more to the key of death and because I cannot explain the key of death properly so that you will comprehend it I will leave it alone. I would have to take you into hell and show you and I have no time because I am deviating from my true cause my poems below.

People this was suppose to be about my vision and I deviated so much that I have to catch up. Don't worry when the time is right I will explain the key of death and this I want and need to do in person not in my book if God permit.

Noah's time is now and you the individual must know this.

Evil has escalated his war so if you think this holy war that your book of sin is not real think again. Right now this war in the Middle East is escalating and we of the west are involved when we should not be. The devils domain does not concern God because like I've said and will say again what belongs to death belongs to death. Sin belongs to death; war belongs to death hence the Greeks told you about Aries – the god of war. Evil must kill because the first act that evil committed was sin – murder. Once you take life that's it because death is born and you cannot escape this judgment because blood is on your hands. Hence sin must shed blood and drink blood. You know this. Just look in the churches. What do they tell you about blood? They say without shedding of blood there is no remittance of life. Meaning if you don't shed blood you cannot have life. This is wrong.

They should tell you the people or individual:
- If you shed blood you are going to die
- If you sin constantly sin you are going to die
- If you constantly commit adultery you are going to die
- If you lie on God you are infinitely going to die. Oh Nelly there's no ands ifs or buts about this. Wooo Nelly for those who writes books of lies – sin and call it THE HOLY BIBLE. Wooooooooooooo Fiya Fi Unnu and I am going to stop here because I infinitely know your deaths and trust me it is not pretty. Vinegar on the cross will be like water compared to what you are going to get. Trust me on this because I now know the meaning about the one jot that is taken from God's words. Wooooooooo mi belly because none of you knew that that warning was meant for you. None of you know that you cannot write books of lies and tell lies on God and get away with it. Not even the renting of your garment and cutting of your

hair can save you because you made nations go astray.

- You made men and woman go to war
- You made humanity sin and walk in sin because of your lies
- YOU LIED ABOUT THE TRUE AND LIVING GOD.
- YOU MADE NATIONS TURN AGAINST THE TRUE AND LIVING GOD WITH YOUR LIES
- YOU MADE NATIONS HATE GOD AND HIS PEOPLE WITH YOUR LIES
- ALL THAT IS WICKED AND EVIL YOU DID TO GOD AND TRUST ME NOTHING ABSOLUTELY NOTHING WILL SAVE YOU IN THE GRAVE BECAUSE YOU WILL NOT BE JUDGED. NO YOU WILL NOT BE JUDGED BECAUSE YOU'RE ALREADY JUDGED IN THE LIVING AND DEATH. YOUR PUNISHMENT WILL BE THE HARSHEST OF DEATH. TRUST ME NOT EVEN DEATHS PUNISHMENT WILL BE SEVERE AS YOURS.

All no let me caps and bold it.

REMEMBER THE GATES OF HELL. THERE IS ONE SPECIFICALLY FOR THE LOTS OF YOU AND WOE BE UNTO YOU WHEN YOU GO THROUGH THOSE GATES BECAUSE YOUR GATE IS THE GATE OF NO RETURN AND THE 24000 YEARS OF HELL DOES NOT APPLY TO YOU BECAUSE YOURS WILL BE

INFINITE. NOT EVEN DEATH WILL WANT TO BE NEAR YOU WHEN YOU DIE. TRUST ME IF DEATH COULD SAY NO HE'S NOT TAKING YOU TRUST ME DEATH WOULD NOT BECAUSE DEATH KNOWS THE SOIL OF DECEIT THAT IS ON AND IN YOUR HANDS. TRUST ME DEATH CRIES WHEN IT HAS TO TAKE YOUR SPIRIT – SOUL.

You made the true and living god out to be a liar and for this you must pay.

<u>God – *THE TRUE AND LIVING GOD never gave man – humanity death. Man – humanity chose death hence we live in sin and die in death.*</u>

Now that I have said this and got this off my chest I have to move on because like I said the death of man – humanity has been confirmed.

I am going to bold, caps and underline this.

<u>***THE DEATH OF HUMANITY IS BEFORE 2032***</u>

You can laugh and say many have predicted and were wrong. You can say this is a scare tactic and I am a flake, crackpot. On this day I am going to tell you this. I don't know or believe in predictions. I infinitely know God and humanities time is up. You can read into this as you like but I am telling you humanities time is up. Meaning the time evil got to deceive God's people is almost up and evil will die before 2032. Now I am going to give you the dream – vision I had.

This is the dream maybe I am deciphering it incorrectly but I know that I am not because of what I have seen in the past.

Many of you are saying if you were of God you would know the cure to AIDS and trust me I got the cure for this but because of laziness I did not get up and write the cure down. I know I failed my guide – the young lady that gave me the cure and for this I truly ask her and God to forgive me. The only thing I remembered about the vision is Maria Punta. I do not know if it's a plant or what but the name Maria Punta I cannot forget. I know Maria Punta is not the name of the plant but somehow Maria Punta is there. And yes she gave me the name of the cure 3 times and no so do not want to be hypnotized. I am not the one to give the cure for this disease. Sometimes when you forget or are lazy it is for a good cause so you leave well enough alone and I have done so.

And no I am not stupid because not everything has to do with money – greed because my kids said I could have been rich but my glory is not in that way. The makers of these drugs know what they are doing and I will not interfere in this because many will have hell to pay and shortly too because the demise of evil is fairly soon.

By now as individuals you must know about the different tropics the Tropic of Cancer and the Tropic of Capricorn. Now correlate it to health – Cancer. Why do you think Cancer cannot be cured and it riddles the body? Cancer refers to the North Pole and Satan – Evil represents the North. And infinitely do not correlate this to Christmas –

December because December is the 13th month of the year. There are 364 exact days in one year and that extra day which is December 29 is for God. December is a holy month. The month given to clean up yourself, your homes everything. From day 1 to day 29 you must keep it holy. The gift of giving is not bad hence the tree – Christmas Tree with its lights donate the life and truth of God.

Look at it this way and know because this is where colors come in. Green represents Life and cleanliness hence the trees clean the air.

The lights represent Life – the beauty of God and true self because without light we could not see in the dark. Nor could we see Life.

The presents you give represents Life the act of true giving because God gave us Life. He gave us food in abundance to eat. Don't even go there because we are the ones to destroy the planet and all that goodness God has given us to eat. So with us giving back to someone else this is good because we are showing God that we care and we are caregivers too. So now you know the truth.

Hence Cancer – the North will always seek to destroy the Capricorn – the South.

Got it

And no I am not spreading lies on the North because your book of Genesis is there as a testament to the truth; the land of God which is the South and the land of Nod which is the North, hence God and

Nod, North and South, Good and Evil, Heaven and Hell.

Anyone tells you Satan was born in December is a liar. The devil can infinitely never ever be born in December – the Tropic of Capricorn.

Know – infinitely know this. Never forget it because you will now have absolute knowledge. Evil can infinitely never ever be born in the Tropic of Capricorn which is the South. Never do you hear me. Infinitely never do you hear me. Know the infinite truth.

Evil is born in the Tropic of Cancer which is the North. Hence evil was in the land of Nod, the North which is the birthplace of all evil not Eden – the Garden of Eden. Now you have the truth.

Yes this why the North will always fight against South. So your so called Jesus could never ever be born in December – the Tropic of Capricorn. Your so called Jesus could only have been born in the Tropic of Cancer the month of June and infinitely not in December.

Yes this is why Cancer is so prevalent in the human body on earth so know your history and heritage – the truth.

Onwards I go because my books overlap each other at times.

This is the vision.

I visioned the earth being moved – the roads in New York had cracks in it. This is the second time this is happening so New York know that you are doing because more destruction is to come and will come if you do not correct what you are doing.

Also in the vision it was like the world was using Canada more specifically British Columbia out West as a dumping ground. When I saw this I said Canada had betrayed God. I was baffled at this and I said to myself not said thought to myself how could this be because I told people to move to Canada if things did not change in America.

This was devastating to me and I said now the earth will for a surety be destroyed before 2032 and this lady – white lady confirmed this and she was telling me and this other lady who is a news caster the reasons why the earth is going to be destroyed before 2032.

In this vision there are two confirmations. People this is the first time I am getting confirmation from a woman because usually it is males that confirm with me when things are going to happen. Because I got the confirmation from a female I am not stressing because I do not know the importance of this female and female newscaster.

Like I said if someone can figure this dream out please figure it out because I truly do not know. When you correlate this correlate it also with the moon – the green and gold moon with the white hue because I think this moon represents death – the death angels and how they come hence this new vision – dream about Canada. Canada is being warned I don't know so truly and honestly help me in a good way if you know.

Here all I have to say is Canada know who you are doing business with because you cannot sell your people short. You have to look after them and secure their future in a good and positive way.

You cannot let anyone come into Canada and use it as a dumping ground for their inferior products – goods because at the end of the day truth must prevail.

HONESTY IS THE KEY
TRUTH IS THE KEY

You cannot bargain your future away because of the Nodites because they do not care who they kill or make suffer.

The Babylonian agenda has always been domination and control and if you let this happen to Canada then you would have allowed the Babylonians to win.

I do not know if I am correct but from this dream the faith of humanity – the world rests on your shoulder and you have to do right by them.

You cannot fail so please secure your economy because if your economy collapses then the entire world collapse. You are the strength and backbone and yes this is a heavy burden to carry but you have to take care of your own.

You have to sustain and maintain your economy. I do not know what else to say because I know not politics or the state of our economy.

Right now God is protecting you but you too have to protect yourself.

Maybe I am wrong like I said and someone can decipher this vision correctly but you cannot under any circumstances let others use Canada as their dumping ground. It is wrong and sinful. Like I said you have to secure your own.

We have time because you have this dream. Do not let God down. We have time to change our faith and go beyond 2132 but whatever you are doing right now is wrong and it will affect the globe in a dangerous way.

I am not getting into your politics but I am telling you what is to come.

Please I am begging you do not betray God because if you do humanity is doomed.

We had 2132 and this date is gone. We can get it back but it is up to you.

I cannot tell you what to do I can only ask and hope that we change this faith.

America has to change its faith as well because this dream concerns them and it is a pity to see New York being wiped off the global map because of their misdeeds and greed.

We have to learn from them and secure our economy. We cannot let our debt escalate anymore. We have to bring our Provincial and National Debt under control.

We cannot spend what we don't have.

I don't know. You don't have to listen to me or take heed and say it's another crack pot speaking but I told you what I saw and I am going to leave it there.

Anyone can ridicule me that's fine but at the end of the day I have done my job. I did relay the message to the best of my ability.

Whether we like it or not global warming will truly unfold and every bank, every economy, every man woman and child will die become extinct.

It does not matter if you are a billionaire you will lose it all

It does not matter if you are the world's richest man you will lose it all

It does not matter what you own and have you will lose it all

It does not matter if you are own every gas station, pharmaceutical company, medical facility, whatever you will lose it all because humanity just got their death certificate and no one can change this once physical time meets up with spiritual time.

We can change it right now but once both times meet humanity cannot change this because the decree is issued meaning it will become final.

For those that now say they are going to sell everything don't because you are not listening to me. I said we can change this decree because physical time has not met up with spiritual time as yet.

And to say I am going to run out and do all the good that I can will not change this decree because you are not truthful to you or God and the others you are doing good to. You are doing to get and you will infinitely never ever get into the abode of God because of this. You are not true. You are a lie and doing as a liar do.

You cannot do to get on any level.

The destruction of humanity before 2032 scares me yes because confirmation is confirmation. It is up to us now.

You can write me off as a fraud and do whatever but I've told you the time of Noah is now and sin needs to come clean because sin will be held infinitely accountable for death –the death of humanity.

Right now as it is sin is using our children to carry out its sins – games and as parents we need to sit our children down and talk to them – tell them the truth. We need to set them right. It's either they walk and live or live and die. Meaning it's either they are with God or against him. Meaning they are for the devil – death. I hope I explained that right.

Right now we are living for death and death cometh and no one can blame God for this because we made it so. We are told the truth and if you ignore the truth then you are doomed.

God is not saying go out there and do this this and this. God is saying clean up yourself, your home, your abode – earth and get ready for him. Infinitely do not put blood on your doors do you hear me. I will repeat. Infinitely do not put blood on your doors like the heathens because this is heathen's way of telling or saying come in take me I want to die with you. Meaning once you are clean, your home and children are clean you will not die with evil because you are clean. As of this day keep yourself and your surroundings clean. If you give truly to the food bank do not stop. Continue giving what you are giving. Do not increase it but continue to give your same amount. When you increase it you are taxing yourself – giving what you don't have and that is a sin and God will not give you good for it. It's the same if you only have good and clean prayers. Do not increase it because the same rule – law applies to you.

If your goodness is tutoring freely continue to do so out of goodness and do not increase it. Nothing changes with God and you and the good that you do.

Death cannot come for Good death can only come for Evil – wicked people – his children. **This is the**

death of humanity is the death of evils children not the DEATH OF GOD'S CHILDREN.

If you are good you need not have to worry or panic when it comes to 2032. Evil has to panic because like I said evil cometh with THE DEATH OF MAN WRITTEN ON IT, which means the death of evil man, woman and child written on it.

Good must now separate from Evil and we have to stop letting our children listen to vile rap music that teaches them the ways of evil – sin

No I am not bashing because the same is said for dance hall music. Right now we have artists glorifying evil and making all kinds of evil signs and we have to stop this. Subliminal advertising is deadly because as humans we don't know that when we see these signs and do them our souls are gone meaning being taken by evil. Evil is the master of lies and deceit and whatever signs evil use it is drawing you – your child into his wicked fold. Once your child is in this fold he cannot get out because evil has him.

Let's put it this way once you sign on the dotted line with evil you can never ever infinitely never ever get out of the fold of evil. There is one way in and one way out and that way is DEATH. Death is the only way in and death is the only way out. Remember I told you about tattoos long ago but did not get too involved in the meaning now you know one of the marks of death – the death of Cain.

But you said Cain had his father's birth mark yes I did but I told you Satan had 3 (three) daughters and each has a six in their foreheads. They are your trinity and please do not correlate this to the triangle. This has to do with the square not the triangle people.

When you mark the body or skin you are desecrating it.

When you alter your body you are desecrating it

All in all what you are doing is accepting sin. I can't sugar coat it for you.

And do not get it twisted if you require life saving operations get them. So if you have a cleft lip that is split at the nose have your operation to correct this. God will not hold it against you.

Don't even bring Transgenderism into this because NASTINESS DOES NOT LIVE HERE.

LIES DOES NOT LIVE HERE

ABOMINATION OF SINS DOES NOT LIVE HERE.

If you require heart saving medical procedures get them done. God will not hold you accountable for sin because you need the operation and you are saving your own life.

The same goes for your child. You cannot ignore their life and withhold important medical procedures from them because if you do you will be held accountable for sin and your punishment will be death because you neglected your child. Yes there are things you can and cannot do but know what you can and cannot do in the sight of God. The best teacher for this is God.

I can only tell you what I know. I cannot tell you what I do not know so God to God for the dos and don'ts of his laws.

And yes this is why we go mad – insane. The brain cannot accept these signs of evil because evil pulls with great force and good repels - pushes.

Know that evil must dominate and control the head – brain. The head is one of the keys to life and death so you have to secure your head because life travels through the head – brain. (Key it this way as I do not want or need to confuse you with the brain and head again. I have to keep it simple.)

Know that what evil takes he will never give it back because there are no givesy backsy when it comes to death.

Evil teaches evil and if your child grow up in evil and learn evil they will do evil.

Right now evil is not worried about the old because evil knows that the old are going to die with him. That deed is done but the deed of our children is not done. Evil need the young to carry on the tradition of evil and his way of doing this is by offering them (our children) all that they want the easy way.

Music right now is the key because music has become the universal language for sin.

Music we say calms and soothes and some do but for others it is an outright sin – abomination unto the soul – good spirit.

Sin must use music to get the righteous cross because whether you like it or not sin – evil has his own brand of music to target the young – younger generation hence evil – Satan was known as a great singer and yes hence the name that some in humanity carry – are born under.

And for those that are going to quit their jobs and say they are going to live in a far away land please don't because this is the destruction of humanity. It matters not where you run because no one can hide from death upon this land.

We are the ones to make this earth become filthy and nasty.

We did not think and like I said one sin affects an entire generation. We know this and have seen this. We talk about this and still we refuse to listen, so the death of humanity should not come as anything new nor should it come as a shock to any of us.

What we sow is what we reap so if we sow bad seeds we will reap bad fruits and this is what we did. We sowed bad fruits and we are reaping them.

We forgot that the earth is like man. All the makeup of man the earth has so if we die the earth dies. If we cry the earth cries. (Rain) If we kill the earth kills. This is cause and effect – our destiny.

We made the choice to follow death so unto death we must go.

I am not here to convince anyone. I have to do my job until I cannot do it anymore and with this book and all my other books I am doing my job.

It matters not to me if you want to continue to walk in sin I've done my JOB and God cannot, infinitely cannot hold me guilty of sin because I did my JOB yes WHAT HE REQUIRED OF ME.

I don't need anyone's soul because GOD REQUIRES GOOD, CLEAN, HONEST AND TRUTHFUL PEOPLE and the majority of us are not clean we live in filth. I am not fully clean but I am learning. What I know is what I know because God made me know hence I teach you and write to you to the best of my ability.

Like I said I am just like you meaning I am human. And no I do not need or want to be like my predecessors – ancestors because God is my keep and evil better not come knocking at my door because evil is infinitely not invited and he needs to respect the laws and law of God and the Universe.

It matters not if sin wants to destroy and kill me – set me up because at the end of the day sin must infinitely die a wicked death. This is my truth because I know the wages of sin is death and sin must die with death.

Sin cannot live and not matter we say a great god is coming to save us this will never happen because LIFE hath nothing to do with DEATH.

Life is life and death is death I told you this and life cannot interfere with death in the grave once your decree of death has been issued and handed down.

God cannot change this. I cannot change this.

DEATH'S DECREE IS FINAL.

Yes God can change this.

No, God infinitely cannot change this because you gave your life over to death, you accepted death. You signed your death warrant – death certificate and this certificate is final. It cannot be change and God cannot go against this decree for me or you.

Everyone knows the WAGES OF SIN IS DEATH BUT TRUTH IS LIFE EVERLASTING.

You gave death your soul – spirit. You did not give it to God so you have to live with your decision - choice.

God must live by your decision. And don't say God said because Jesus is not God.

Don't even say yes he is because all I have to do is send you back to your book of lies and deceit.

Now tell me if Jesus was God how come he does not have the keys to hell – death.

Read your revelations and tell me who has it?

If you are a child of God, God gives you everything for you to see and know. You cannot deceive nor can you tell lies.

What you see is what you see and you have to tell what you see.

I've seen many things but do not know who to tell hence many of my books are outdated because they are still in lalaland. Meaning they are still on the internet and no one has bought them yet.

If you are reading this book then yea you bought one.

Know that sins pay is sins pay and God's pay is God's pay and for God to change the rules – laws for you or me to accommodate us he has to and have to change the laws for sin to accommodate sin.

He cannot change it for you only and not sin. Right is right and fair is fair.
God cannot change my sins to accommodate me.

What about sins sins come on now?

We are the ones that are not faithful to God and look at what it has cost us. It has cost us our lives. We are to blame for this no one else but us.

Yes sin gave us a way.

God gave us a way also but we accepted the ways of sin and now it is almost too late. I say almost because we can change this. Anyone that knows time know this. I know this. God knows this so chose your faith wisely.

The question I now ask is why?

Why let it get this far because of sinful and wicked people?

Why destroy ourselves for sin when we know that the wages of sin is death.

Truly tell me why?

We talk about the ark but none talk about how we have become so sinful that it hurts God.

No look at the beautiful planet God has given us but because of wickedness and greed we let evil and his people take it away from us.
Dear God what have we done?

What have we done? What have we truly done unto you?

I want to cry but I have to hold back the tears because humanity will now have hell to pay and I truly know why. It is because of our sins – sin.

Yes God's people will be saved from this destruction because this destruction is the death of sin and his wicked and evil people on the planet. Good life must prevail and live free and true to God and for this I must truly thank God because I know he is preparing a place for his good and true people.

Yes now we will truly know that the WAGES OF SIN IS DEATH and no matter the true messengers that tell you you kill them, massacre them for evil and evils ways.

You cannot turn form God and do all this and expect God to continually bail you out.

You cannot sin and expect to get right all the time. This is sins way not Gods way.

Sin is always looking to get right for the wrongs he has done. As humans we do this as well. If Cain ran from the truth what say you?

When we do wrong we lie about it – run from it then expect to live in peace – live a good life. This cannot happen because the sins of man – humanity has spread too far. I've sinned but I cannot run from my sins I have to own up to them.

I cannot allow and refuse to allow sin to have victory over God – The True and Living God come on now. No My God is my God and this earth was not created by evil it was created by God – Life. Death cannot have life because death is dead – hath not life.

God do not deal in death so when we let people give us over to death we too are wrong. We can no longer betray ourselves because of death – we are infinitely wrong, hence my vision of betrayal by Canada when it comes to God. And yes maybe Canada is going to betray me hence I saw this dream in this way. And no people I am not God. Maybe this dream is for me but it matters not because I know the place where I must be. I am just waiting for God to release me from my decree meaning the hindrances of evil.

Like I've said and will say again I am not worried about evil and his people because all evil must die and die soon. I am concerned about God's true people because they are the ones to be saved by God and trust me it is not many given the billions of people that reside on the earth.

What evil is doing is wrong. It is not right and God cannot maintain and sustain evil any longer because as it is because of evil we can hold God accountable for sin – the sins of evil. Meaning if you ask him cleanly and purely, honestly and truthfully and if he does not help in a good and wholesome way we can hold him accountable.

God did create the earth and evil has no claim to it. Evil has no right to the lands of earth.

Hell is evils domain and if evil wants to live evil must create a planet and domain for his people. Yes this is hell but hell cannot be on the planet earth hence evil has its time to live then it must die like I've said.

God has given evils people a way out but if evil do not want this way we as God's children – messengers have to leave them to their sins – evil ways.

Michelle

Onwards I go because I have so strayed.

Now let's get into the Dark Side of Me

TABLE OF CONTENTS

Prologue	Page	31
Poems of darkness	Page	32-169
Poems of Boredom	Page	170-197
Worries of the World	Page	198-234
Concept of Humanity	Page	235-249
A Little Fun	Page	250-253
Odes of Lust	Page	224-278
Infatuation Explanation	Page	279-280
Poems for Lovers +	Page	281-293
Ode to Robert Nesta Marley	Page	294-308
Stones Thrown at Jamaica	Page	309-359

Prologue

Within our lives we are faced with darkness and loneliness and it is out of this darkness and loneliness that I wrote this book.

Many of the works are dark and will offend some if not make a lot of you angry especially the stones thrown at Jamaica. It is with good intentions that I wrote those stones and do hope Jamaicans on a whole will see where I was going when I threw the stones.

The mind is a fascinating program that can use us at will. It can and make you conceive anything. It is a powerful tool that has eluded mankind for centuries. It is more powerful than a computer, the ultimate doorway to God but yet it keeps us from this doorway. Keeps us at bay.

Hence the darkness within me and you.

I do hope that out of my darkness you can see the light and gravitate unto the light within the darkness.

Michelle

The Master of the Game
The lies just keep getting better and better
Greater and greater
Tell me something
When will it stop?
When will your deceit stop?
When will people learn the truth?
The bible is not based on God
It is not based on Satan but on you
But it is funny how people associate Satan to you
Associate Satan to your half truth
Manipulation of the truth
Your lies are profound
Therefore you have manipulated man forever
You cannot tell the truth
But lie perfectly to shift the blame from you
Making them believe it is Satan
You have manipulated history to suit you
Manipulated man to do your very will
Mislead so that man will follow you
Worship you
You take the truth and use it against man
You are the master planner
Master manipulator
Master deceiver

We kill for you
You have become our drug dealer
Government
Church

As for me, since I know you
You are holding me back from my full potential
Get out of my life and never come back
Get out you are not welcomed here
You are not welcomed in my temple anymore
Consider this your eviction notice

You have been evicted
As for your trolls of liars and deceivers
Your vipers living in the den of destruction
I banish you and your master to eternal damnation
Banish you to hell
The true hell outlined and build for you
Your master too
A hell constructed by the Supreme Being

Get thee from around me
You're all evicted from my surroundings
Evicted from around all my family
Permanently

Take your master with you
Take the dragon with you
Take your lies, your pain and suffering with you
Never ever come into my space again
None of you are invited in my holy temple
Around me and my family
Go get
I rebuke all of you
Get out of my house, my life
My family's life

Out of all our lives

I bind you to your kingdom
Seal your pit and gates
By the will of the true Supreme Being
By the will of the King
By the will of the Supreme Being
You will hurt no more
By the will of the King
By the will of the Supreme Being I cast you out of our lives
The lives of others
I open their eyes to the truth and open the door of the King – the True and Living God
The Most High who is the Supreme Being

The truth will be known and Revelations will be revealed
You must fall
You must be destroyed
Utterly destroyed

Tortured Soul

You have pulled the wool over my eyes for far too long
You have pulled the wool over my eyes for the last time
You have held me back in life for far too long
Caused me pain and suffering
Put my family on the brink of starvation
On the brink of being on the street

There is no love within you
Everything I have asked you have treated me unfairly
Treated me worse than a dog
Left my life in chaos
In utter disrepair

I have no job to go to
No job to help feed my family
Many of us are scrounging by to keep a roof over our heads
Clothes we cannot buy
Furniture needs replacing
Everything breaking down

Prayer have become my stay
A stay filled with unanswered questions
A stay filled with confusion
Personal destruction
Unwanted demons

You have given me your ring
But a ring don't mean a thing when the one you love hides from you
Leaves you to die
Leaves you and many like me without hope
Scorn

Don't need lies in my life
Need my God to be truthful - honest
Need my God to be my true friend

Tell me something and this time answer me
How can a God that says he loves you leave us unfed?
Leave us with questions trailing behind us

What parent would do such a thing?

What mother or father could not care?

What mother or father does not want what's best for his or her own?

Tell me what parent gives without truth – true love?

What parent cannot truly love his or her own?

All my life I've been looking for true love
A mother and father that loves me truthfully
A good God-Creator that can truly love me back
Be honest and truthful to me
When do the lies stop?
When will you open your eyes again?
Open up to me and listen to my plea
The way I feel
My honesty

As in my search I have found nothing but pain
Suffering
Many tearful nights
Darkness around me
Nothing
Emptiness
Now I know the one God we look to is truly not there
There has to be more

There has to be truth out there

More times there's no paradise to look to
All I see is darkness
Lack of a home
An empty life
A life of unhappiness – emptiness
Boredom
A life of struggles and hardship – pain
A life filled with regret and guilt – sin

Looking beyond my surroundings
I see hatred
War and strife
I see people fighting in the name of religion
Fighting for their King
Fighting for a God that is not truly there

I see false hope
Dreams shattered
Lies from heaven above
And I wonder why a God of true love would unleash hell upon the people of planet earth
I have to wonder when the hatred in heaven and earth will stop

When will the two unite as one and forgive
Truly forgive each other and stop the nonsense that's been hurting us for centuries
We need to move on to the next realm
When will we stop hindering each other?

Truth lies within
None is better than the other
We need to stop trying to prove each other wrong
Stop moving in different directions

There is one Supreme Maker, Creator, and Designer that loves us
How to find him we just do not know
But we will if we keep on looking
Jesus found him and so can you. But then again truth is Jesus never existed. His story was taken from Greek Myth and if you've read Greek Mythology you would know – yes you would put the pieces together and know.

It's been over six thousand, six hundred years according to man but truth is evils time is 24000 years and the end is near.

This fighting must come to an end because there is nothing to prove
Think and see the destruction around you

See the destruction of this planet

Where can we run to?

Where will we hide?

There is no place like home
Concede and do the right thing.

Forgive and learn but never forget lest we go right back in the same situation if not worse again

Michelle

Driving Back the Enemy

I am fed up and tired of the lies in my life
Men that are ghosts that is around me
They are like shadows
Are shadows that protect?
But do nothing to help your well being

Men that watch
Lurks in the dark
Men that drives your life down
Men that scare and keep others from coming around you
They are like live vultures, living demons

Well to all of you this is for you
You are not needed
Stop hindering my life
It's over
Get the hell away from me
I need positive growth in my life and if you are not here to help me leave me the hell alone. Don't come around me anymore

In my eyes you are like unto a:
False prophet
False witness
False pretender

Liars and deceivers and I truly don't need you around me
You are like unto a thief lurking in the dark to steal my life – my soul – my spotlight – my glory

Stop, truly stop holding me back
Stop stifling my life
Don't need a ghost
Be gone I am rid of you
Get far behind me
Better yet find your home
Not mine
And take your heavy load
Heavy burden with you

Michelle

A Little Talk

You just won't stop will you?
You just don't give up do you?

Who the hell do you think you?
Hindering me and my life

Who do you think you are?
Interfering in my progress
Holding me down
Keeping me back so that I have nothing

My family is important to me
I will not let you use me anymore
I will not end up in the streets because of you

Who do you think you are coming into my home and making a mess and mockery of it?

Get out! Get out! Get out
Get the fuck out and leave me the fuck alone
Don't need demons of sin – death around me so stay the hell out of my life and away from me you are not invited so stay out and get the hell out

I rebuke you, I rebuke you, I rebuke you.
In the name of God I rebuke all evil from around me

Evil stay the hell out
Read the sign
It says:

"ALL EVIL KEEP THE HELL OUT OF MICHELLE'S DOMAIN. YOU ARE INFINITELY NOT INVITED IN HER SPACE NOR ARE YOU INVITED AROUND HER AND HER FAMILY. SO STAY THE HELL OUT OF HER LAND AND TRANQUIL SPACE."

Who are you anyway?
No one cares
You died a horrible death
That's your doing not mine

My life is mine
Not yours
You have no right troubling me
Interfering with me

My Collective – The Dark Side of Me – Part One

Stay the hell away from me
Do not let me tell you again
You are not apart of my life or home
You are not clean
You are filthy and dirty
Why would I want someone like you?
You lived a life of lies and deceit
Whored around
Caused me shame
So stay out
I don't need you
No way
No how
So forever be gone clown

Michelle

Goodbye

Take your dirty hands off me
Take your dirty meddling hands out of my life
Take your lame ass game out of my life
Take your broke ass away from me.

I've loved you
Supported you
And all you've done is break me down
Caused me to lose it all
Caused me to have ill health
Caused me to cry
Caused me nothing but utter shame

You're not love
You're just another broke ass man
An abuser that takes and takes
You take what you want to feed others
Leaving me to beg
Even starve

Take your deceiving love elsewhere. You're not needed around here
Take your false love away from me
I refuse you entry
I throw away the key
Take back your ring
Because I refuse to support your broke ass no more
Go on get, you lying no good so and so – SOB

Michelle

Tell Me

Yes I am getting strength now
So take your damned noose from around my neck
Take your traps out my way
Take back your damned key and leave me alone
Don't need your crap in my life anymore.

How dare you do this to me?
How dare you mess up my life?
Then turn around and say you are married to me

How can a person claim they love you?
Are married to you and mess up your life
Destroy you
I am physical
You are not
What sick joke are you playing?
What sick game are you playing with our lives?

Can you ever come clean?
Are you even capable of total honesty?
Truth
Or even true love

I have lived with your lies all these years
Put up with your crap
And this is how you repay me
By letting me live worse than a pauper
By showing me things to come
But yet holding me captive

A prisoner in your dungeon
There is no warning with you
Tell me what kind of monster are you

Tell me
Tell me what sick games you are playing – like to play
because your sick jokes are all played out

Tell me do you sit and watch like the days of old?

Sit and watch as we crash and burn
Is this a gladiator sport to you?

Do you sit and watch while people pollute
Rape the land
Kill sensesly
What is your view?
Your take
Or do you not care about our existence

Do you not care about the lives that are being lost upon the planet earth?
Do you not see the willful destruction and abuse of the land?

Do you not care that humanity is destroying it and leaving it to die?

What manner of evil is this that humanity has to suffer at the hands of the evil ones?

Evil hath time to destroy but what about goods time?

Where is the time for good people that try not to bask in sin?

Know and learn a person that loves cannot truly give nor can they truly love because there is no truth in them.

A person or God that truly loves truly gives – truly cares. Hence love cannot be true if there is no truth in you.

Michelle

Evil Spirits

We are living in a nightmare
The threshold between the physical and spiritual

What we are in the physical determines what we are in the spiritual meaning the goodness we do determines where we go in the afterlife – spiritual

Evil cannot show you who resides in the spiritual because evil does not know
No one knows
Not even I because this sight is not given to man because God's abode is God's abode and no man or woman of sin can enter there

I have yet to see the prophets of old in my journey guiding me – educating me because to be truthful God have no prophets he has messengers, angels – guides too.

In my travels I have seen the man called Jesus and to be honest that was a sick joke played on me by my subconscious, the evil guides around me because I infinitely know Jesus never existed. Yes this is religion – the source we rely on hence religion the source of all religious lies – newsprints. Once you are walking true with God then you will see the lies of the spiritual world – you will see evil in its true form.

Hell is no place to be
Shit it's no place for you or me
No place you want to be
Confusion is hell and hell is confusion a lot of babbling hence the tower of Babel – Confusion
Confusion confusion
Confessions confessions hence the devils domains teach you of confessions – confessions of your sins – bad and misdeeds

Repentance you will find none only spirits wondering without a true home
Wondering spirit yes wondering spirits all baking in hells true domain
Have mercy, have mercy, have mercy upon my soul and you will find none – no mercy given to your distraught and pitiful soul.
Have mercy you will cry even louder but none will hear you because God would have fled – truly gone away

The voice of God did cry out in the wilderness for you to save yourself from this eternal and everlasting flame but like the days of old you ignored your warning signs – you did not learn – listen

Have mercy I am sorry you will scream I cannot take hell and the pain no more but your mouth will be shut closed because no one wants to hear your pleas

You had the time to live but you gave up life and lived for death. Death is your calling now. It is your home – paradise

Yes the spiritual world is a mess for the wicked – the evil at heart
It is now your home of no rest – peace
Your home of the living and walking dead
Your home of true Cannibalism
Your home of ions – negatively charged Atoms
Your home of no peace or happiness
Just a place to roam and roam
Yes this will be your true home
Your home of Doom and Gloom

If you dream know the truth of dreams – visions because they are not always true
Truth is you have to decipher your dreams
Dreams are not always exact – right because as we Jamaican say dreams don't always walk straight – right

Some come to you as truth
But they mean the reverse sometimes
You have to be careful you are not deceived in this spirit world because there are good and bad spirits and there are more evil spirits than good

Power is in abundance in the negative state of dreams because you are given things and you have to be infinitely careful what you are given and what you accept because not all are true. Some are infinitely evil.

Evil is extremely strong and powerful in the dream world
At times you don't know who to trust

The spiritual can be painful
You have to be careful who lets you in and who you let in because in the spiritual world evil is real and it dominates everything that concerns evil living meaning physical evil – wicked people hence spiritual wickedness in high and low places

Death and sorrow is not pretty is not pretty because death is serious and death do not play games
Be careful who you talk to because evil is strong
Death is just a step and a knock away
Be ye careful of death – evil and be strong in all that you do for Life – God.

Michelle

Petition for the Dead

There is nothing to forgive
All there is, is the pathway to good and evil
The pathway between the here and now
Good and evil

Spiritualist claim
Men, women and children claim to:
- See and talk to the dead
- Enchant the dead
- Invoke the dead
- Worship the dead

Those are their truths
What they know and can do

I would love for one of them to take a walk in my world
Walk in my shoe
For them to recant and tell me what they see
Bet none of them have seen what I have seen and lived
What I still see and know of the dead
Death and evil

Bet many cannot walk in my shoe
Can't walk in the shoe of others like me
I have to wonder if they would go crazy
Would be scared out of their minds
Bet you think I'm crazy
Death is no joke
Neither is the dead

Trust me there are no offerings here
Just the truth
Can you handle it sucker?

Michelle

The Mind

Many come and go in my life
Many try to scare
Many are lost
Without a home
Many have something to say
Left unfinished business to resolve

I see faces clearly
Some pleasant
Many unpleasant
I see death clearly
Death sees me
Knows me
Is afraid of me
But in time I know hence I walk on the road of life and infinitely not on the road of death.
I know my time to go but death cannot take me – he did not make me because I will freely leave my shell- body when it's my time to go. Death will not pluck me out of my body. I will come out of my body at will and go to my Father – the True and Living God that made me.

The mind is full of tricks
It plays evil games
Uses its tricks to convince you
Alter our perception of the truth
It makes you do its will
It can even kill

It just takes one incident
And we are lost in its tricks
Lost in the follies of the mind
We get caught up in its game

Whilst it deludes you
Smiles at you
Causes you shame

Many drift in and out of illusion
It's like a well crafted magician
The master of the game
The master of the hunt
The clue to God and the universe
The clue to creation
Knowledge of God
Paradise
But yet with all this we still do not know

We are deluded by this monster
It makes us believe that there are monsters in closets waiting to get you
It makes you afraid of the dark - night
It makes you believe you are not beautiful
Makes you want to be like others
It makes you hate yourself – others
It makes you have inferiority complexes
It makes you feel weak
Unloved
Uncared for

Aah the mind
A well oiled machine
That controls our thoughts – will
It conditions us and sends out chemicals in the right area of the brain to keep you fed – distraught
It traps us in our thoughts
Beliefs
It makes us believe what it tell us
We let it tell us what is true
It has us believing in lies

It holds us captive in its little square box until it has
no more use for us then it lets us die

No man knows his own truth
No man can tell you his own truth
Even know the truth
Everything we know was taught
Even the God we believe in was taught
Nothing we know is of ourselves
True
Truth

The mystery of heaven and the planets will always
be a mystery because we know not the truth
Because no one knows the mind
Therefore it is fair to say
The mystery of God no one knows
God is not based on your truth
Your knowledge
It is based on what you were taught
Taught by others
Your thoughts configured by the mind
The stories of the ages – centuries foretold long ago

We hear voices
That voice that says he made the atoms
Well what about combustion
Light colliding in the darkness
Refurbishing
Creating new life
Everything is recycled
Worms eat your carcass when it dies
Bacteria protecting the body
Basic Science
Renewal of Life – the darkness and the light
The process continues

Darkness is the key to light
Light is the key to darkness
Both are equal
Male and female joined
One union joined by two souls
One union pulling and tugging
Dividing
Expanding
Manipulating
Multiplying
Adding

He she
She he
He he
She she
Whatever the union
There must be no deviation
No confusion
One soul – spirit

But yet many cannot see in the dark
Many cannot comprehend it
Basic bible knowledge
Man cannot comprehend what he or she cannot see
Man cannot comprehend the scope of Nothing
Cannot comprehend the One because if they knew they would know there can only be Two, a union of the cells on a molecular level – the male and female Lion – Lyon on a biological scale – human level. They cannot comprehend the Elyon – the she Lyon – Lyon of Judah – the house of God.

Man does not have the knowledge to what he does not know hence he cannot comprehend God because he knows not God

He cannot comprehend the universe because he knows not how the universe came about

He cannot comprehend life because he knows not life or how life came about

He cannot comprehend truth because he knows not the truth

He cannot give life because he knows not life hence he cannot give life he can only give death – the death of life

The mind is in the universe
The universe in the mind
Open the trap door take a peek
All you will see is darkness but in fact the darkness is light. The light in the darkness and the darkness in the light

Think about this
The mind does know this but yet it continues to confuse, play tricks on you. Yes use its little mind games to get to you

Michelle

Darkness

The God we know
The God we love and trust does not act alone
Everything we have been taught and learned is a lie
The God we know cannot create by himself but is this truly God or is it the beginning of man – human life – the union of egg and sperm?

"***Let us make man*** in the image of God created he them

Male and female created he him"
The book we come to love clearly states this
But yet contradicts this
Lie to us about the fornication of man – humans

God will never act alone
Cannot do things by himself or herself
He is painted as a liar and murderer
Is this truly our God or is this the truth of evil – human life – humanity?

Questions arise
We read falsely
We are blinded
Become fools to a system that traps us in its web of lies – deceit

We cannot take or hear the truth
We were conditioned this way
Conditioned by men
Enslaved by men

We play the blame God
The God game
Therefore we accept lies
Live our lives by lies
Truth elude us
False hope shapes us

Lies defines us
Mould us
Kill us

When will we realize that we cannot do anything by ourselves?
We cannot live by ourselves
Do anything by ourselves

When will we stop the killing?
When will we stop the hate?
Prejudice
Racism

Everything was put in order
Confusing and contradicting isn't it
But without space there would be no time – human time – spiritual time for the wicked

Space defines us
Control us
Give us a space to live – area – country
But with all this said, this is not who we truly are – not who we will become

My bold statement makes you fume
Outraged
Make you want to lash out
Makes you want to harm me
Aah the follies of man
Now think of Jesus and what his own did to him
Think of Jesus and how his own fumed
Sought to kill him
Are you not acting like them him?
Is Jesus not Satan the first begotten of the dead – meaning death?
Is he not the son of death – Zeus?
Contradictions contradictions but know the truth Jesus – Zeus represents the spiritual dead hence you worship and

praise him as your God but in fact he is a dead god – the God of Death

There is a master planner
That is whom we should seek
Laws and instructions are given
His subjects need to follow

God is just a mere servant for some
He's a subject
Employee
But the Supreme Being
Is leader
Fashioner
Knower
All

The Supreme Being eludes us because there is no supreme being only God – Life
The All - Allelujah

God is beyond our comprehension
Beyond the realm and scope of the mind
Because in the mind this perfect being does not exist

This synergy of light and darkness combined
This beacon knows it all
Is the All

We call him God but ooh what a mess
There is no him or she but pure unrefined energy

Darkness is forever

Light is not. Because within the darkness there is a great power – force that cannot be seen
This great power – force knows the truth but yet BLUE the color light blue eludes me.

Dark Blue is that powerful but Light Blue and White combined is the key to salvation for some but to those who know knows that this is the key to the destruction of all evil. Yes this is why we have the Blue and White Nile. It cascades through Egypt because back in the day it was the source of great power and the source of great evil. You should know this hence you have a window into my world – the world of Blue and White – the Blue and White Nile not Blue Ivy but blue and white not the distortion of colour – evil.

Yes many must fall – ball but this is death – the life we choose

Death must come but not in Blue and White but in Black and White. Not the colour of skin but the colour of hue – material colors – the colors of death – destruction

Therefore man cannot live forever in what we call the light
What we call the flesh

Confusing yes
Contradicting yes but this is the dark side of me
All that I do is to get you to think, see and know

Truth exist in all and all is in all

Michelle

The End

The spiral of the end is near
Global economies collapsing
World drawn in cataclysmic chaos

Global warming
Financial ruin
Rain and fire looms
Earth devastated

Greed has finally taken its toll
The bell rings
Wall Street collapse
The downfall of the upper class – the super rich
The downfall of money laundering and foundations used as safe havens
Ah yes the end of greed – the greed of man - humanity

Revolt everywhere
Starvation upon the land
Cannibalism out of hand
The doom of earth
Fall of mankind

Rebirth
New genesis
A new beginning but when
Greed still stains the land. Blood still flow because man kills man.
Ah yes the ark almost gone
The infinite death of man – humanity

Michelle

RAGE FOR A LOST SOCIETY

God my anger is beside me this day
Please forgive me because goodness fails me

I am so pissed off at life – society

Humanity have and has gone too far with their evil and abominable ways and I am beyond anger. I am fueled by disgust and hatred – rage

God how can a man have a sex change and call themselves a female and vise versa? God the anger this stirs in me is beyond me

This blatant abomination of sin goes beyond my scope of reasoning and is beyond disgusting – worse than Satan and all that he has done.

God it is far from me to tell you what to do and I know changing sex is abominable unto you but if you ever let vile and disgusting abomination of sin – no not sin because sin is too good of a word for inhumane no not creatures because creatures are better than them. Just disgusting cesspools like them enter your kingdom – abode it will be you and me.

God no one has the right to pollute and change what you have done – given them

How dare these things
They're not even human
Satan is better than them

God I know we have a choice but it boils my spirit/soul to see what these things are doing

God don't even put them in the same kingdom as Satan because in my book and like I've said Satan is better than them

Satan is good compared to them

At least Satan knows he a damned liar and deceiver but what are they? They are nothing but vile and disgusting abominations of shit worse than sin

God I get angry you know that and I vent but I have never felt so strongly about anything. God come on now. I said I will defend you and I have and I've used strong words. I am infinitely particular about you but this one takes the cake it stirs me the wrong way in more ways than one

No God I am not going to hide my conscience but if you let things like these enter your abode you might as well give Satan and his band of agents – demons an all access pass into your kingdom.

MICHELLE

God I know we have sinned against you and I have but you know how I feel about genetics – life

God where is the ethics in society today?
Where is the ethics in man – humanity?

Where has integrity gone God?

Listen Lovey – God I have skeletons in my closet and I have to face these demons one day but what gives man the right to undo what you have done?

What gives man the right to call your creations wrong?

Who are they?
Who the fuck are we?

God man changing themselves into women and women changing themselves into men this is worse than an abomination of sin and you cannot allow sins like these to continue to happen. Nor can you allow sins like these to enter your abode

God I cannot and will never comprehend transgender bullshit. This goes against humanity and more importantly it goes against creation and what you have created.

How dare these things say you made a mistake when it comes to genetics and creation?
Who the fuck do they think they are?

God do not bring homosexuality into this because true love can be between male and male and female and female. This is so in the spiritual world because

I have seen it so no transgender thing can use this. God there is truth in love because true love is pure. Being transgender is wrong and you know it.

You do not favour this. This is an abomination unto you. I know this because your emotions flow through me at times

You told me to write and you yourself have shown me things – made me feel things I don't think any ordinary human can. You made me feel things emotionally as well and I refuse to lie to people to please anyone including you

I refuse to be fake
I refuse to lie and I will not lie about my emotions or yours

I more than infinitely and truly love you but I refuse to allow humanity to go on sinning this way

Yes humanity have a choice in what they do but you and I both know that some things they have no choice in and they cannot do

You cannot hide this from them because this goes beyond disrespect. They are challenging you and your creations

God transgender is the new Sodom and Gomorrah literally and this is where raining down fire and brimstone applies literally.

God man have and has become disrespectful and insolent. You may be able to sit back and take the crap and shit man is doing to you but I refuse to.

Natural occurrence of man evolving into women and vise versa is fine. There cannot be any medical intervention in any way (absolutely none) to change males into females and females into males. Natural sex change without any form of medical and non medical intervention and when I say non medical I mean taking any form of herbs to alter state – the state of your body is also not fine.

You do not have an issue with natural sex changes meaning if you are born a male and at a certain age you turn female. This is fine because you have allotted for this it is natural. It is when people go out of their way and alter themselves medically you have a problem with and yes I have a problem with this too.

Certain things we just cannot do nor do we have the right to do this. There should be laws banning transgender operations because these men are not women and the women are not men. None of them should be classed as females or males. This is infinitely wrong.

They are worse than abominations of sin and like I said I put Satan over them.

God I do not hide my feelings from you and I am telling you the truth. As vile and disgusting Satan is I value Satan over them and that's low.

God I make no apologies for my words – statements but these things should not be considered humans – amongst the humans of this earth.

Sodom and Gomorrah is for them belongs to them hence they are the true Sodomites of this land – earth

God we have sinned against you and we are still sinning against you. I am no exception to this because I too have sinned against you.

Shit Satan and his demons have sinned against you but Satan have never disrespected you in this way. Satan despise and hate you God, his people despise and hate you. They hate your people – children but he's never disrespected you like this

He's lied to you yes but his lie is not disgusting compared to what these things have done and are doing to you.

God I truly love and respect you but I cannot hide my conscience – the way I truly feel about these vile and disgusting things.

MICHELLE

God I cannot tell you what to do but I hope there is no forgiveness for transgender things – men and women who go out of their way to change their birth.

God a male child is a male child
A female child is a female child and no one can have sex changes via medical anything to change their sexes.

You cannot change your records to accommodate humanity and anyone who do this is wrong

God why will humanity not learn and know that nothing in the spiritual can change and the life you live in the physical determines where you go in the spiritual

God each human being have and has a birth and death certificate and you cannot change their birth certificate accommodate them. Your birth is recorded as male if you are born a male, female if you are born a female because this is how it is recorded in your record books

No one can change their death certificate because once your certificate is issued and physical time catches us to spiritual time this certificate becomes final. It cannot be changed no matter how much good you do in the physical. So because of this no one can change their birth certificate but yet some acts of abomination do so in today's time

God today I am petitioning you and any country that legalize things – say it is okay to have sex changes to reflect another gender I do hope you lift your hand of protection from that country infinitely and let them go down like Sodom and Gomorrah of the bible

God I feel so strongly about this and this is the first time I am going to tell you to do something naughty – wrong but God make the land desolate worse than Ethiopia. God I would rather petition for Ethiopia and Satan before I petition for these vile and disgusting things

God any land that legalizes things lift your hands of protection from them. Do not shield that land anymore God but instead let Satan use that land for his own. God do not treat those lands any different from Sodom and Gomorrah. God nothing that they do favour it, do not favour them or the land.

Do not even look upon the land or favour their prayers.

God I've always advocated good and for me to ask this of you or even say this you must know how I am hurt – truly hurt by these things because they are not people, they do not respect you or even care about you

Who are they to defy you?
Who are they to defy your law and laws?

God truly forgive me but I am truly hurt yes angry and I am letting my anger show. God truly forgive me but when it comes to you and all that you do I become truly defensive especially when it comes to you

God I know how hard you work to maintain us and all we have done is spit in your face and tell you you are wrong.

We can't even bathe ourselves properly but yet we disrespect you

We know not the beauty of life but yet we take life from you

We pollute the earth without knowing that the sins we do – commit affect the earth in a negative way

Tell me God why should I live with these things at my door when I know they will cause the land to crash and burn?

No God I will not advocate violence against them but I will advocate that they get nothing from you. I will advocate for you to take away your blessings for any land that give these things rights – human rights because they are not humans. They are liars and deceivers that are willingly causing humans to go to hell and burn.

No land is blessed or will be blessed with these acts of sin. Now I truly know why it repented you to form man meaning give man life because at every turn – angle man disobey you and infinitely disrespect you.

When do you draw the line God? When do you truly draw the line when it comes to man – humanity?

MICHELLE

Lovey when does the madness end?

When will you truly walk away from humanity and let us truly eat the bread of our sorrows?

Lovey forgive me today because I made my anger surface again but this time I asked you to do something that is wrong please forgive me?

God I respect all that you do and I am very particular when it comes to you

Yes I am over protective of you and need what's best for you but I am sorry for asking you to do wrong – commit sin – wrong

God what humanity is doing towards you is not right and I know I have to contain my anger but God how can I when humanity deface and defame you?

God you don't deserve this. You don't deserve the disrespect of humanity

Lovey and God I am truly sorry but you know what humanity does not deserve you. You've given us so much and look at what we have done to this world and you

God what is the use?

What is the point in clinging on to humanity when can't do right by you?

We challenge you
We do all manner of evil against you
We falsify you
We spit on you
We've caused your creations to die
We anger you

Man everything in the name of sin we do.

We give sin life – keep sin alive and when it comes to you we destroy you – do everything to kill you

Lovey I've done you wrong. I've done a lot of wrongs and nothing that I do can change my past – what I've done to you but to have people – things changing their gender via medical procedures go beyond my scope – the scope of sin and life

God I don't know anymore

I just hope and pray that soon you will let your true people find you. God I hope and pray that they will learn to respect you and praise you meaning give you true thanks

God please rescue your people. Protect us from what is to come but truly let Satan deal with his own people and for those transgender things let true evil deal with them because Satan is evil but he is not true evil. There is a greater evil more pure and diabolical than this man we have come to know as Satan.

MICHELLE

God have mercy upon me and forgive me of my sins

God please be there for me and defend me

Be my strength when I am weak
Be my shield at all times

God the road sometimes gets rough but you know me. You know how I truly feel and you

God I know I have asked you to do wrong but please forgive me I was wrong

God I went against my words – your words and for this I accept guilt – punishment because I did wrong

I know I am not strong as you God and I am sorry if I've allowed sin and true evil to laugh at you. It was not my intention so please do not hold it against me

In future or in the future I will try to contain my anger but I am not promising you anything. I will defend you don't get me wrong but I am not sure if I can be mild – gentle

God you know my mouth and like I said I will defend you – stand up for you. Lovey let's turn the tables just a bit.

Tell me something how many times have you stood up for me?

How many times have you shown me your loyalty?

Don't even try it because I can't count them so I rest my case because you have been with me through thick and thin so why shouldn't I be there for you through thick and thin?

Forget it I know you can speak for yourself. You have a voice and you can defend you but today I am speaking for you meaning I am defending you – taking up for you

Forget it you can chastise me later infinitely much later but you are my Boo, My Baby – you are True – The Truth

You are infinitely right so why shouldn't I stand up for you

I cannot be ungrateful to you maybe others can because they don't remember your goodness and kindness and I cannot be like them. I have to be different. I have to defend you. No I will not use evil but today I made evil take hold of my thoughts and for this I am wrong – guilty. God I cannot change what I've asked you to do and will not change it because I have told you the truth of how I feel. If I changed my thoughts and words then I would be guiltier than sin and I would have lied to you.

Lovey despite my ways you are my true King and no one disrespects you not even me.

MICHELLE

God let my children find you and never ever infinitely never ever let any of them become a thing

God if any of my children or off springs meaning grand kids and future generations ever become a thing – transgender anything I will infinitely never ever forgive you and I will charge you for sin because you know how I feel about them – these abominable things

God creation is sacred. None of us know the value and pleasure – beauty of life but yet we try to undo it

God what right does any of us have to undo what you have done? None of us know the time and effort that you put in everything but yet we seek to undo what you have done

Lovey man cannot tell time – the true time
Man know not how each element came into creation but yet we claim to know by falsifying your records

How dare us?

Who the hell do we think we are?

Tell me God who the hell do we think we are? And yes I am yelling at you.

How can it repent you to make man and you are still putting up with the shit that man – humanity is offering you and doing unto you?

How can you say you are love when you can't even respect yourself?

What we are doing to you is not right. Yes I comprehend the scope and greatness of your true love but what about your integrity God? What about your integrity?

We can't even clean ourselves properly but yet we falsify you.

God how can we be clean when the air we breathe is polluted and the water we drink we dump human and animal waste in?

God we cannot clean ourselves so how can the one to save us live clean when nothing around us is clean – we have polluted everything

Well you know what God fuck humanity and its dirty and false ways because the smallest of atoms you created it. Atoms man have yet to discover and see so humanity is nothing more than bullshit a pack of liars and thieves – wretched deceivers.

We can't even love right but yet we claim to know you – love you

We can't even fuck right but yet we claim to know life – give birth unto death – unclean kids - unclean everything

What the hell do they think – we think?

Climbing atop each other is love it's not love it's shit – exercise for the heart because none of us know life – true life that is in the egg and sperm

They know not the life in the water of these cells but yet they say they know life

They claim to know life but know shit. Some lie and say it takes 72 hours for a sperm to reach the woman's egg and impregnate her but it's a pity they don't know the truth of life because true life does not take 72 hours to begin – life happens right away less than a day.

Yes 72 hours the three days of sin, the three (3) sixes – the three (3) daughters of sin

God man know not time this is why they guesstimate and estimate because all they think they know they know nothing and trust me this nothing is truly nothing it isn't and cannot be something because this law does not apply here.

MICHELLE

God cool me down
Cool me down tonight God because my blood boils

It is hot
On fire

God I cannot dismiss you like humanity I have to stay true to you and defend you

God despite my unlawful ways I am truly depending on you to work things out in a positive and good way for me

God I value quiet – privacy but it seems like the devil has come back to ruin me but I refuse to let him

Lovey in time things will be different truly different because truth is I did not listen. I should have known what you were trying to show me

It's a lesson well learnt and trust me I will not be making the same mistake a second time with them

God how could I not see this coming?

How could I not pick up on what you were showing me?

Wow was I gullible but it's good to know before it's too late.

Yes God the way is clear right now and I thank you for showing me many things.

Lovey this man with his kids the man in the pink shirt rescue him for me and make everything be alright in his life

I don't know who he is but he needs stability with his wife and kids. Yes he's left her and she wants to see the kids and he won't let her because of what she did

God pink is good. I also know that pink is prosperity – good but you cannot let a broken relationship harm these kids

God I see the harm – the car hitting one of the children because the little boy was running away and you cannot let this accident happen God you have to secure this child for me and the sake of him – this child

God work things out beautifully and good
Work things out right and just for these two. Once again God I do not know who this man and woman is but you have to help them

You cannot let the kids get hurt because of them God. You can no longer sit idly by and let families be torn apart by greed – vanity

These children did not ask to come into this world their parents conceived them so they should not be caught in the crossfire

God let the better parent get the children. God chose right for these kids because humanity have and has gone astray
They have forgotten about the kids. They have forgotten that their children feel hurt and pain

God not because two parents are not there it does not mean that they cannot be good parents. Both parents can play an active and positive role in their children's life

God not because a parent is separated or divorced does not mean that life is over for them their children

God there is so much a parent can do and I hope this man and woman do it – do right by their children and be the best parent they can be

God all too often when a relationship has ended or is over we use the children as pawns to get back at each other and this should not be. I learnt the hard way so therefore I don't do it anymore.

My children know as well as see for themselves which parent is truly there for them – truly love them. They know who the better parent is

God like I said I do not know these people but you truly need to intervene and do something

You truly need to help the children because the husband – ex-husband is as stubborn as a mule. He does not budge when it comes to certain things – especially his kids – children

MICHELLE

God this day is not going right for me

God the pitfalls are there and so far today I think I have fallen into the trap – the pit because anger has and have taken a hold of me

God my son has pissed me off

How can he be upset over something that does not belong to him?

God this is not the way I am raising him but yet he has this cumungin attitude. God it's nasty. You cannot be red eyed over other people's things. It is worthlessness on his part and I cannot stand it nor will tolerate it in him or any of them. When they do this are red eyed it's as if I as a parent is worthless practice worthlessness

God why me?
Truly, why me God?

God how can he grow this way? I've talked to all of them about this. They know but yet my last one refuses to listen

Yes I yelled at him and I do not feel bad. I hate and despise a worthless attitude and being red eyed is worthless a worthless attitude.

MICHELLE

Oh God help me to get through the night

Help me to see clearly and know my way

God in all that I do please do not let my sinful ways – thoughts affect you

God forgive me today
Forgive my sins

Help me to clean my dirty ways
Help me to purify me

God give me the strength to walk in your good way

Give me the strength to stay strong

Give me the strength to live another day – a good and healthy life with you

God in all that you do do good unto me and bless me in a good and prosperous way.

MICHELLE

The thoughts of my mind runs wild and free
The thoughts of you defy gravity
It's beyond insanity

The floor hath no room for what I want to do to you

Fire and desire cannot explain it
Lust no that's not it

Maybe it's because I am trapped in this haven of love – fire and extreme desire

My thoughts of being one with you
Sharing your bed

Brazen am I for thinking this way because I truly don't even know you

Have never met you and although I am longing to touch you I can make you my desire. I could and can become absorbed in you

Yes these are my foolish thoughts

My thoughts of being with you

Shame on my part but yet I am hoping to find you.

MICHELLE

My thoughts are dark – painful
My needs wanting sometimes shameful

Confusion sets in
My thoughts of you wrapping your long legs around me

I can feel the heat no not the Miami Heat
Forget the Jamaican heat you too

The coldness of your caress
No warmth in your touch

Is it me or is it you

My ideas of love is not what it should be

Ah yes too much thought of you.
My wanton desires – never thought you'd be so cold.
Man did I ever misunderstand you

The longing in your eyes
The fears of sins – past history gone by

No one understands you but I do. They see you but yet in their eyes they see their own desires – greed

Pity that you cannot change the coldness of the heart – you

Pity you live in fear and please forgive me if I misread you.

MICHELLE

Okay sweetie how well do you know me?

Can you frame me?

"Frame you," he said as if in disbelief because he truly did not understand.

"Yes frame me. Can you frame me?"

"No I can only frame your picture. I cannot frame you."

She looked at him then walked away. She could not believe he was that dull boring. Her thoughts were outside the box but he was still in it – inside the box and that disturbed her.

She was fun and adventurous and there was no way after knowing this, hearing what he said could he possibly satisfy her. She needed someone that could not see a box but could see a vast universe while they played and basked in true love.

He had disappointed her now but that did not matter she was gone through the door.

She had left on impression on him but he did not get it she was never going to return – never going to come back so he waited for her like a fool. Now years later he still thinks of her and lights a candle beside his door. He knew the love lost a love he truly never knew.

MICHELLE

"Wendy"

"Wey yu want?"

"Pegasus"

"Yu a flyin asse or di hotel?"

"Noa but mi a di stallion wey a go ride yu."

"Stallion fi who?'

"No you"

"Ya right. Mek mi tell yu sinting mi a stagga bak. Mi bruk dung stallion cause yua igle juby no jacky. Fi yu lickkle two furlong caane help mi so ride and cum again."

"Wendy"

"Wey yu want?"

"No yu"

"Couldn't me because yu caane angle mi. Di lickkle two minute a no chups not even wet. Pickney bouy fi mi roune one sits at 45. Minutes that is and since yu a two minute man mi no want yu. Cause when mi cum yu done and trust me disya funeral will be one for the record books so don't pick up what you cannot manage. Mi done but mi no_____"

MICHELLE

"Wendy tell me something you a si di lickkle two minute bouy?"

"I've upped the game"
"Laude oh no tell mi say yu gaane American?"

"No found me a nice little man"

"Him can manage fiyu bumpa?"

"Noa but mi slow it dung fi im"

"Yu slow it dung fi im dat no mek no sense"

"Noa but im ave di money"

And on that note ladies and gentleman I am going to leave it alone. The mind is going too far and I so don't want it to run away with me in a bad way so let's truly leave it alone before I step it up a notch and go buck wild with the things I can say and do.

MICHELLE

Sorry was spelling my name wrong there because the mind is so in tune with my outrageous and naughty side. Come on no Ooooooh's you truly know me when I get obscene and crazy.

Michelle

"Hey baby you look fine tonight. Can I buy you a drink?"

"That's alright I am fine."

"That you are pretty lady that you are. You are more beautiful than the galaxies and stars"

"Once again thank you but truth be known I am waiting on someone."

"He's a lucky man." Topping his hat to her

"Indeed he is," and she gave him a beautiful smile and she was gone. Finding a table she patiently waited for her special someone but she didn't have to wait long before this little man sat down beside her. He must have been about four foot two.

"Sorry I'm late my queen."

"You are not late my king you are right on time."

"He was fair game"

"True but I have the bestest of them all. He's a giant in my book – the true love of my life and hey you know me when it comes to pick up lines."

"But you are beautiful more beautiful than the galaxies and stars.

"I'll better be because you are it in my book you are my galaxies and stars."

MICHELLE

"Will you stop pressing me for information?"

"Come on Dee I want to know who he is"

"He's someone I met in the grocery store"

"Okay he's married – has someone?"

"He's a long time friend"

"Ah ex-lover. I guess he was not that good in bed for you to dump him"

"Actually he was that good"

"So why dump him?"

"Don't like the cheating and whoring kind"

"All men cheat"

"Not the one I've got now"

"You ain't got any hence you are single – all alone"

"Got a man he does not cheat and I can put all my money and trust in him and on him and come out the winner."

"Yea right and the world is going to come to an end today if not in 20 years because knowing you you have a man stashed away and for the record he does cheat. That's what men do best they bed hop from one hole to the other, bed hop from sheet to sheet."

"Maybe your man but my man does not cheat and I can and will stake my reputation and all my worldly possessions on him"

Including your multi-million dollar bank account?"

"Every last penny"

"Trust this man that much"

"Infinitely because he has my back and I have his"

"So if I was to prove you wrong, prove to you that your man cheats you will give me everything you own and have?"

"Yes"

"It's on" And all that her friend did to find this mystery man and prove her wrong failed.

"Give me a hint friend. Tell me who this man is because I have looked and search and I cannot find this man and you know me I cannot fail."

"You have failed and will forever fail because no one can prove God wrong. No one can prove God to be a liar or a cheat. See God is my man. My true love and he will never infinitely never ever cheat on me or fail me."

MICHELLE

"What can I say to you to make you understand me?"

"You can start by telling me the truth"

"I've been telling you the truth. You're the one to not understand."

"My friends saw you with him. Here's the proof you were kissing him."

She holds her head down because she could not believe his friends could do such a thing. She did not know his friends watched her.

"Tell me something is this not you in the arms of another man?"

"Yes it is" She could not lie to him nor did she want to because she lived by her truth and integrity.

"So you are not denying it?"

"No but I can explain."

"The proof is in the pudding. It's over between us. You are nothing more than a common whore and I don't ever want to see your face again. Get the hell out and to believe I trusted someone like you. Get out," throwing his wife out of his life. He did not want to hear any excuses all he wanted was the truth and she told him the truth. He did not want to hear her explanation he had the proof his friends gave him and that was all he needed. His friends had his back looked out for him at least so he thought. Letting his anger take control of him he sealed his own faith because he had the truth all along. He just forgot about her photo shoot.

Complying to what her husband said she moved out and a couple of weeks later her face was on the cover of a leading and cutting edge fashion magazine. The headline read clothing giant Calvin Cheung snags a beautiful plus sized model.

Flipping through the magazine he saw the pictures of his wife kissing another man.

Yes the pictures said it all now his wife was gone and he was the one to look like a fool. He was the one to be all alone. His wife was gone. He did not want to hear her explain.

Rushing home he dressed in his Sunday best. Hoping his wife would forgive him for all he had done to her he rushed to her mother's home.

"God I know I hurt my wife but please don't make it too late for us. I was angry- wrong and now I know the truth. Please God help me to make it up to her. I did her wrong she did not cheat on me. I am the one to not listen. I chased her out of my life. Please do not make it be too late for me please God because I've been so lonely and miserable without her. I can't pretend I do need her."

Driving to his in-laws place he inquired about his wife but she was gone for a month. She was busy doing a fashion show.

She had to occupy her time. She had to move on with her life. Her husband had given her a terrible blow – wake up call. He had trusted his friends more than her and valued what they told him above her.

She was faithful to him and he knew this. He knew her going out and coming in but in love there are doubts and lies. There is no truth.

We all love for some reason or the other but when you truly take a look true love can never be there because true love does not cheat. It cannot cheat because it's pure – natural.

No money compares to true love because in truth we grow and truth cannot die it can only live.

So as she looks back to the past she stopped herself and smiled.

"Ah mama you are so right one hand cannot wash it takes two. The two must be in unison – unify. One cannot love true and the other love both must truly love. Both must know truth and live for truth – live in truth."

Going home she called her husband. "You came by to see me," was all she said.

"Yes I wanted to apologize and say I am sorry for hurting you. I messed up please forgive me. Please give me another chance to prove my love to you. I know it won't be easy for you to trust me again considering what I've done but know that I am truly and infinitely sorry for hurting you."

She smiled at herself and although it pained her to say this she had to say it anyway. "I'm sorry Lance but I can't take you back. In all that I have done with you I've always been faithful and true and it is because of this I cannot take you back. I have to be faithful and true to me."

"Baby I love you and want you back. What can I do to prove to you that I am sorry? I never stopped loving you. I am going crazy without you. I can't eat, I can't sleep I need you in my life. Baby please reconsider and come back in my life. Be my wife and love once again."

"But the truth is you are not true. Goodbye Lance I will always love you true." She hangs up the phone because deep down she knew all that she did would affect him. The money she would be making he would not be able to handle it. He would not support her but instead he would dissuade her from doing what she truly loved to do.

She knew in all that he did he would still run to his friends for advice instead of going to God and his wife. She knew his friends would fill his head with all types of lies and evil thoughts. They would still do what they do – watch her and give him a play by play.

No she could not handle that so she stayed true to herself and prayed that God would find her the right man – that true and honest someone.

MICHELLE

We build our lives, our hopes but yet lies have taken shape – fold

Everything is based on false dreams – the perseveration of false gods but yet I have to wonder sometimes if my God and True Love is real

I question myself as well as question him based on fears – feel – the lag of time meaning the distance of time

All that humanity would do to destroy self was written in time long ago but yet no one knows the truth that this earth has become the devil's playground – stomping yard – domain

When you think of Noah's time Sodom and Gomorrah it's here today because humanity have and has become vile – perverse

Every abominable acts of sin we do but yet there is no law – no laws of God that is known to man

Men write but God has become as one of the dead
He is dead to some

God what do you truly say?
What is your true laws not the laws of men?

How can humanity listen to you and obey you when books that were written and stored in Egypt have been destroyed by man so how can anyone say they follow your laws when they know not your laws?

How can we say we praise you when we do not know you?

God truly tell me what are your laws? Don't be afraid to tell me – let me write them down

God this morning I have not love true love in my heart because I feel abandoned by you

I don't know this morning because you refuse to listen to me and do that which is right – correct

God I will not back down from you and yes I am prepared to go head to head with you when it comes to the truth. I've told you you cannot allow sin to destroy humanity. You cannot allow sin to destroy you. You have to tell us the true truth. You cannot let us live our lives based on lies and if you let this continue then you too are guilty of sin. I've told you this.

Everyone will have a right to hold you accountable and judge you for sin and God don't even use the bible because you know the bible is a pack of lies. You cannot justify yourself based on lies that men wrote. Lies that we teach and preach, lies we knowingly tell on you. God what these people preach and teach is about you and today God I am tired of defending you because you are not listening to me. You are stubborn as a mule. You refuse to budge and defend yourself.

God I truly love you but my spirit is downcast as if I have failed you in some way.

God how important is humanity to you?

How important is life to you?

I blast you; quarrel with you but today I have no fight left in me. I feel all alone on this battlefield – the devil's playground.

God no this is not worth it. Truly humanity including me is not worth it because I cannot understand why we would build weapons – atomic bombs to wipe out nations and yet have no remorse.

God we talk about the devil being a liar and a deceiver but truth be known the devil is crap compared to the shit humanity put you through and the crap that we do

God we humans are the true devils.
We are true and pure sin

No God just look at it
Look at all that we do

We live in sin

We live for sin

We conceive in sin

We die in sin

All that we do is sinful because we are the ones to destroy – commit murder – sin

God how can we blame Satan when we are the true evil ones?

We build nuclear bombs, atomic bombs to destroy nations. We humans have done this

We spy on other nations

Devise chemicals to kill ourselves by using them in our food, medicines

God tell me how can we be pure when all we do and live for is to kill – destroy?

Please enough with the choice today I don't want to talk about the choice we made because I will get angry and I will lash out at you for creating pure evil because you knew this would happen.

You cannot hide from it any longer.

You have to stop running God. I am tired of the games God – the distance in time. I did not chose this faith it was chosen for me and I say that choice was wrong because I did not need to sin. I did not and do not need sin in my life.

Yes my mother didn't know nor did my ancestors to a large extent. God growing up I did not fully know but the truth was there but she hid the truth from us hence hatred developed amongst family.

God I see it, heard it from the horse's mouth but yet you permit this so tell me God how can you escape this judgment – my judgment?

With you it's see and blind, hear and deaf and this attitude is wrong. Cannot fly with me and it does not fly when it comes to you. You cannot alienate humanity from the truth because we are not an experiment. We have life and no I refuse the first begotten of the dead bullshit. This is revelations

time I agree but it's time to reveal the truth and you cannot continue to let evil imprison us.
God stop living wrong and start living right. You cannot hide the truth from us anymore you are wrong

I refuse to give you right when you know that you are wrong

Today I am calling you out. You have a choice God I am giving you that choice – you have to choose now because you have a responsibility to man – humanity.

You can truly stay by me and truly love protect and shield me or you can walk away and pretend as if I do not exist. You have a choice because I am truly fed up of the evils of this world – fed up of sin.

I need my true life back God. You cannot take this from me. You cannot take my true life from me. You cannot leave me alone to defend you. I cannot pretend that I am happy when a lot of times I am lonely. Fuck this loneliness now God. I am tired of it. It's like I am a fucking prisoner living in a dead world. I feel like I am a captive of sin. I can't go forward or backwards it's as if I am stuck in a doomed world of utter sin – death.

Tell me God how can anyone be sane – live?

Truthfully God if you truly love us then why leave us?

Yea yea the cleanliness but once again on this day I have to question your motives – integrity. And don't even go there or fume because I have the right to because today my spirit is not right it is in the wrong mode.

It's in the question mode and yes the lonely mode.

Ah well God you know me. I have to question you because we cannot be truly happy each and every day when each and every day all of humanity dies a little bit more.

Forget it God I refuse to buy love I'm not a damned prostitute. Fuck that why should I buy love. I may be lonely but I am not desperate. I've told you I am looking for true love that true and honest man that can truly love me. And how the hell did buying love comes into play?

Buy love come on God but that's a whole new avenue – ballgame so don't get me started. Too late you've hit the nail on the head so here I go because I am so going to go there.

MICHELLE

God why did you do this to me now? God Mr. Vegas She's a Ho is playing in my head

God come on how many of us have run from man to man looking for Hot Wuk. Yes yes yes I know hot wuk was not what I wanted just move the W and replace it with F because we are all prostitutes. Hey God been there done that meaning had more than a couple of men on my belt trying to find the right man – the right companion so no I am not going to take myself out of this because this is my past experience and not my present.

Men don't laugh because you be a Ho and Prostitute too. Need I remind you of the notches in your belt? How many of you buy women and parade them around like high class train wrecks – yes prostitutes?

No no no fuming because this is the dark side of me here.

Hello shut up need I remind some of you of your countless porn stars. Forget it many of you had the Playboy, Playgirl and Hustler magazines. Oh ya I forgot about the top and middle draws with the countless porn DVD's.

Come on don't let me open the draws for you. Need I remind you of the stash under the bed, in between your mattress, hidden in the back of the closet. No come on not under the pillow. Shit boy inside the bathroom stall is just plain out nasty. Oh did you try nuky on the bathroom seat? Sorry had to ask because that question came to mind.

Was it fun? No I'm thinking painful no not for you her. Ooh man here I go again and no this time there's no sex toys because some of you have gotten too kinky and sick for me.

The bondage and whipping shit plain out sick – freaky.

Some women are just plain out nasty. Yes I'll tie your ass up. No baby with the panties. The handcuffs, whips and chains that's bondage – slavery. Not into that shit. Don't want to relive my ancestors' ordeal in some man's freaky shit. It's just sick fucking sick. Someone whipping you like a slave fuck that.

What are you telling me you took the slaves off the plantations and bring them to the bedroom to be degraded even more. Fuck why don't you just buy the man – oh I forgot some of you do that already. Service Jockeys well that's what we call them back home.

Yes for some the rent a dread

Oh well I guess prostitution will never die because anyway you look at it we all do it already – cheaply.

MICHELLE

God it's amazing the shit that some women do for pleasure

God what message are we sending especially to women that are abused

When and where do we draw the line when it comes to freaky shit?

God women are not slaves and no men are not slaves either. You know what I just don't know because my knowledge is just developing and I know some of the things I have written needs correction but God when I have achieved full knowledge and over standing let me amend them. Full truth is essential and I know you will give me full truth and comprehension.

There is clean sex but then you have the freaky shit. I guess to each their own and I just do not want to see this debated because some women have to go through hell at the hands of some vile and disgusting human no not humans but demons. Demons that they have to lay down with and do shit with them. They don't have a choice because these cesspools of shit have taken their dignity and self respect.

Yes I have a lot of pent up anger towards sin and trust me there's a lot more where that come from and this is why I drill it in your head God to separate good from evil as well as for you to respect yourself.

Do not let good commune with evil because the more we commune with sin is the more we commit sin and die and yes the more vile we become.

God to hell with the Ying and Yang now man shit you need to separate us. You need to help us live a clean life. You cannot keep us trapped in the cesspool of sin any longer.

I am fed up of asking you and you blatantly ignore me. What the hell is wrong with you God?

Why do you persist on keeping us tied to sin – evil?

Look at this world God and tell me truly tell me you condone what is happening to humanity?

We are killing each other for what a portion of hell a place that hath no life

God not because hell hath no life does it mean we are to turn earth into it – hell.

Why God why would anyone want to go to hell when they know they are going to die there – there is no life there?

God I'm tired because we cannot live clean we made sure of that. We've polluted everything including the water we drink. So tell me if all the sources are dirty how can anyone live clean – be clean?

MICHELLE

No God truly tell me how can we live clean when everything we do is dirty?

I will forever ask if the head is dirty, how can the body be clean?

I've asked you this God but yet you've failed to answer me maybe it's because I know the answer to my own question but it would be nice if you did answer me. I will not ask you again well not at this time but I will ask you again but today I ask and ask you now if the water we drink is dirty – polluted, air we breathe is polluted – dirty, food we eat dirty – polluted, prayers we give dirty – polluted how can we be clean? Live clean?

Everything is polluted God so how can we be clean? More importantly God how can I be clean? Am I not dirty also? Are you not dirty also?

Don't even bring up the I told you to write a book story. Clean is clean and you cannot change this to please me or anyone. You know the truth cannot change to suit you or me, anyone for that matter so don't bring the I told you to write a book analogy up because you know I am right – correct.

No no no God no excuses I don't make them for you so don't make them for me. Yes I am trying to make my life clean but I am not fully clean God because I live in sin and amongst sin.

The frontal lope of my head is hurting me so I am going to leave well enough alone God but think about what I said. You know right from wrong God and despite my ways you know I have to question you. I wouldn't be me if I didn't.

God maybe it's because I need you to be sure of me and I don't want or need to fail you. I don't want to be like the other messengers that after a while turn from you. I've been through too much in my life to abandon you that why I tell you to hold on to me and let me cleave truthfully and honestly to you.

I know the friendship that we have and I can't give that up it is too beautiful. You have shown me so many beautiful things in the beauty of life and I need this beauty in my life. I need this beauty for others too and this is why I tell you too that we need to know the truth.

God we are not babies anymore. You cannot let us grow in lies anymore. You have to let us grow in the truth.

Whether you like it or not God if we don't change our dirty ways we will all die meaning we are going to die if we don't make that change.

Good people will die and you cannot allow good people to go down with evil – sin and his people. It's not right it's wrong and don't give me any bullshit by saying you cannot interfere. If you say this then I know you are not capable of the truth you would be liar therefore you too would be guilty of sin and evil would have won – triumph over you.

MICHELLE

God what is the point of life when we live for death
It is beyond me as to why we write and tell lies – deceive for the enemy

God if the bible falsify you what should man do? The bible is evil. It is evil's book and has nothing to do with you but yet humanity go to their graves believing it's true without knowing that the bible is a lie it is evil's book.

God how can we know you? Truly know you when the very books we read and hold in high esteem tell lies on you – deceive humanity?

God evil has stolen your identity. Evil is a thief – an identity thief. We know this but yet evil has turned everything around on you. You are depicted as the ultimate sin – pure and utter evil because you bask in sin and blood offerings.

You steal

Hey you're even a murder

God when the bible teaches all this, tell me why should man – humanity want to know you?

Tell me something God if we are taught to steal and kill will we not grow up to steal and kill?

If we are taught that you kill will we not believe that you kill?

If we are taught that you favour one race over the next will we not believe this? So how can we be clean if we are living in the den of thieves?

How can we be clean if we ourselves are thieves?

Many believe you're a murderer God. You kill and this is your legacy – the legacy of you depicted in the bible and in the hearts of all humanity. This is what we read. We are taught this and God you uphold this because the men that wrote and write these lies say they are and were divinely inspired. Their words come straight from you.

God you're a murderer so why should anyone trust in you? Isn't this what we read in the good book – the book that has enslaved and corrupted all of humanity – this book we call the holy bible.

There are other books out there but God come on now you are a murder someone vile and disgusting because you are sinful, you participate in sin. So if you participate in sin why shouldn't we? You can't hold us accountable for sin because you are sinful this according to the bible and what I read? Hey the bible said you send prophets to kill – you were at the head of their arm don't blame me God it's in the book. When disaster strikes humanity calls it an act of God. Wow Hon I never knew you were pure and utter sin – evil.

Damn God we've put you lower than low

How do you feel?

Do you feel right?

Are you hanging your head down in shame yet?

Do the tears well in your eyes?

You are a murderer and a thief. This according to man but yet you have mercy on man – have pity for man

God when did you become a murderer?

Shit when did you start drinking blood and bask in the sins and atrocities of man?
When did you become like man?

Wow Lovey with all this said why should humanity trust you?

Why should humanity have faith in you?

Why should we try to know you?

We've humanized you

Well no we did not so I stand corrected we've put you on the same levels as psychopaths on death row. Yes it's a shame but that's what you get when you play the lying game meaning the lying games that human's play on you.

God how do you live knowing that humanity has and have turned from you?

How do you feel knowing that we live for evil and die for evil?

How do you feel knowing that we are doing all that is evil for evil?

God what is goodness when all that we think is good is evil?

God come on now can evil be mended – change?

God when does the lying stop because we do lie when it comes to you hence everyone say we have to die to reach you.

God no one have to die to reach you. When did death become a part of you?

Listen Lovey in all that we do we all have a birth certificate and a death certificate and no one can change these no matter what we do. We cannot change the way we are born or the way we die because these two are factors in life. One is life and the other is death and no human or spirit can change this – this is law.

MICHELLE

God when did you become death worse than Satan?

God when disaster strikes we say it's an act of God wow. Hey we made you the murderer okay we have to live with it not you. No you too because we are lying on you.

God when did you become the death angel – the avenger of death – evil?

God I don't know what to say but why do you take all of this? Why do you believe and not know?

Well you know humanity believes. Yes I know humanity can be saved and yes the one to save humanity must be clean

Lovey you are going to have to create a new and special universe for this person to save humanity because the cesspools of sin is more than sky high

God she will have to be an exception to deal with the nonsense of humanity. God she will need a special force field and bubble around her – surround her

God she will have to be strong and more than clingy to you if she is to succeed

Oh well God good luck when it comes to man – humanity you and her are truly going to need it.

MICHELLE

God from the past to the present sin has had its fun
Man – humanity have always been its game now we live in captivity
Live as slaves – demons

We've become slaves to the political system
Slaves to the religious systems
Slaves to schools – all schools of thought

We've becomes slaves to man
Slaves to women
Slaves to sin
Slaves to false and devious gods

Don't get me wrong education is key because knowledge is a gift from God it is humanity that do not use this gift wisely.

We use our knowledge to kill, dominate and control and in all that we do we falsify you by telling lies on you

We have forgotten about freedom
Truth and Honesty

We live for greed
Love the lies of greed
Live and love to lie

The sun and moon no longer shines in a good way thanks to the hearts and souls of man. Both have retreated meaning both now work in unison for the death of man

Good and Bad
Positive and Negative
Ah yes soon they will all be gone bye bye thanks to man

MICHELLE

God I cannot go by the bible but yet it is said thou shalt not kill

God I've told my children that you don't mind if they killed and eat meaning if they are hungry you would not mind if they killed a chicken, goat to eat but not a human but God isn't this a double standard for me if you require all life back?

Yes I know everything hath life down to the fruits that we eat, the air that we breathe. God I know this but as humans we don't know what's right from what's wrong.

I know chicken is the food of choice in the spiritual realm – world because both good and evil use chicken – cook chicken well bake and fry chicken. I know the meat of swines pigs – pork is unlawful to eat because pigs represent evil – demons – voodoo worship. Pigs represent filth and nastiness – evil in the spiritual world.

Dogs are unlawful to eat because they represent humanity – males and females but males specifically.

Cats are just plain out evil they are like pigs in the spiritual world hence they are used in pure evil

Horses flying horses represent a specific race within the black race well some of them don't think they are black because they are of mixed breed – Black and Indian and although they say they don't have Indian in them they do because they too speak the Babylonian tongue a dialect of Urdu otherwise known as Arabic. Yes they are the ones to fall from grace remember the biblical account of Satan falling from grace meaning it is said he fought against the angel Michael and was cast out of heaven. The story is incorrect – inaccurate because Satan never resided in heaven meaning sin cannot and was never in God's abode. God is not dirty nor is he sinful now put it all together because I can't do it all for you. (Yes people hence the bible added fallen angels. They were a specific race of people on earth that fell from grace meaning God no longer recognized them because they mixed their seeds with the devils seed hence they are no pure – apart of God's good race – pure race of people). Ah just look to Ethiopia, Israel, Somalia, Certain parts of the Caribbean even my homeland.

The Bear represent strength and protection. The Bear also represent humanity and true love, the protection of the female that it truly loves. The Bear I am baffled by because I cannot comprehend the bear. It's not elusive but there is something I cannot put my finger on. Maybe it's the coldness and confusion of this given race as if they are looking for something that they cannot find. To me they are misunderstood but this is my perception who knows maybe one day I will learn the full truth about the Bear if I'm not wrong.

God all these things I know but when it comes to life I am confused because everything hath life but yet we kill and eat and like I've told my children in the book dedication unto my kids it's okay to kill and eat meaning eat an animal. God this is a double standard that needs to be addressed and clarified because of the thou shalt not kill rule – law which is confusing.

I know it is a sin to kill a human being this is outright unlawful and wrong. This is sin and it is wrong. No one can dispute this. This is law and this law cannot be changed to suit anyone

Well God what about the animals and the trees?

The air we breathe. Yes I know the air is recycled.

Oxygen and CO_2 people but animals they too hath life. Trees hath life what about them? I know the trees clean the air and help the moon to cool the planet down. I know if we cut down one tree we must plant two or three trees in its steed. God I know this that we are to replace 1 tree with 2 or 3 if we cut one tree down this is the law. We are to replace what we take but God how can we replace human life and animal life?

How can we replace that which we have eaten?
Once that life is gone it's gone. There is good life beyond the spiritual threshold but beyond the spiritual threshold I cannot see

I know the operation that good people must undergo before they move on but beyond that operating room – table I do not know

Yes I've seen the Crystal City. I know there is no city of gold because you do not love gold but silver – shiny things is what you love hence silver is a part of our makeup – genetics – hair but still God I am confused as to life. What constitutes life because everything hath life – everything grows?

Today unconfuse me God because this weighs heavily on my soul. I need to free my mind because I know it's not all meat that is lawful and good to eat nor is it every plant – herb that is lawful to eat as well

I also know it is not every race that is lawful to lay with hence we are not to mix our seed with certain race – races.

I know – infinitely know that the laws of clean and unclean do not go for animals alone it also goes for humans hence Eve did not listen and laid with an unlawful man hence we have certain unlawful races that dominate the land. Hence we must know which races are clean and which races are unclean. This has nothing to do with skin colour for those who are going to use the colour scheme it hath to do with the heart – the goodness and evil that you do – family and ancestral family do.

One race basked in pure and utter evil while the other basked in good – the goodness of life hence you have the land of Nod and the land of God. You have to know who the Nodites are and who the children of God are. And yes a black person and a white person can be a Nodite because black people still reside in the land of Nod until this day and remnants of the black civilization can be found in break off lands in the land of Nod. Do your research in a good, true and honest way and you will find the truth. Look beyond control of land – meaning colonization because black history go back to the beginning of time long before the forming or union of egg and sperm – Adam and Eve.

God many things I do not know so please clarify the gift of life for me

God yes chicken is the choice of food – meat in both world but why chicken God?

Why not fish some other meat?

Certain animals represent humanity yes and therefore they are unlawful to eat but why the chicken? I know this is beyond my scope – knowledge maybe one day you will tell me the true truth.

A part from chicken being baked – cooked I have not seen any animals in the spirit world being cooked. Nor do I see them (animals) living amongst these spirits – human spirits. I have not seen animals living in the spirit world.

God I have never seen one. Like I said some animals represent human life – people but as for the spirit world I've yet to see animals living there meaning living amongst spirit people – humans in the spiritual world.

So God please before I move on to higher life please clarify the true meaning of life because this I need to know and all of humanity need to know too. We know a lot about death but when it comes to life we know nothing.

MICHELLE

My Collective – The Dark Side of Me – Part One

God why is it that we seek to dominate and control?

God what makes one race more superior over the other?

God with all the fighting and killing that we do how can humanity say they are going to see you?

God I am going to say this but do not take it the wrong way and I know I've asked this question before.

If all humanity thinks this way meaning kill and worship – go to church and worship how can you be right?

Are you not wrong God?

Come on now God we sin and worship you so how can you be right – clean?

Are you not dirty so therefore you cannot be clean because we made you dirty so therefore you are unclean?

You are unclean meat – food
You are unclean spirits – demons
You are sin – death – pure evil

You cannot deny this God because we made it so and you have accepted this because there is no good life anymore. Just look at the churches and need I bring you to humanities book of lies Genesis. Remember in Genesis the second creation not the first. Remember when you made Adam and Eve you did not say they were good. Your creations were good but when it came to man – humanity they were not good meaning Adam and Eve was not good. God I know humanity can read into this and take this the wrong way but I know the truth because Genesis is the beginning of sin and not good life.

This is where sin got life because sin was death – powerless

Through Eve sin was born got life and if humanity truly looked into it there was no Adam in the Garden of Eden just Eve

Satan – this man we call Satan did live he was the first for Eve hence Adam. She gave birth to three (3) daughters – the daughters of sin hence the trinity.

Good and evil combined brought forth evil. Evil life because evil is strong it pulls and destroys hence good and evil – WILL. Because of this union – the union of good and evil – the interlocking Star of David man can do both. He or she can do good and evil meaning one minute we can do good and the next we can do bad – evil. (For those of you that are confused. The triangle facing down represents evil – the male sex organ, no scrap that. Down is evil – up is life. Oh man that's a poor explanation. Okay forget the star of David yes the Mogen David. Take your Christian Cross. The cross represents man – the living soul of your bible. The little part at the top represents the head of man – each human. Now when you turn the Christian Cross downwards meaning the little head is facing downwards this is pure and utter evil. Once the cross is turned down you are worshiping evil – pure evil. You have become evil in its truest form. And yes if you have sold your soul to evil the downward cross is what you represent – carry around. Satanist cannot represent this because not all of them are pure and utter evil. The true representation of evil is the Christian Cross facing downward. This is why Christians have the cross paraded in their churches. It just means they are evil – but not fully evil – they follow evil. The cross represent man not God. Therefore, no one in the Christian faith represents God or worship God. They worship man and represent man. Yes this goes for the Baptist, Roman Catholics, Protestants, Muslims, Mormons you name it. They all represent man and the worship of man and not God).

But but but. There are no buts and ifs. This is the full truth hence the devil sits at the head of every church hence you have the cross roads – cross – railway track in every church across the globe.

This is why I tell you not one of us represents or know God. Now you know the story of Noah. God is the ark and humanity is sin – meaning we know not God hence we follow sin to our deaths.

We refuse to come out of sins domain hence good die with bad because despite the truth we would rather follow sin.

Everyone thinks that God is a religion when he is not. All cannot be one because All is many hence Allelujah and Allah. Yallahs to be exact – meaning God is all around – everywhere.

Through religion – all forms of religion sin – evil is able to dominate and conquer. It preys off the good and innocent. Without good evil cannot exist it will die and remain so – dead.

God this is why you told Eve the day she eat of the fruit she shall surely die and she did die because evil is death it cannot change it is XX meaning female in life and in death. She became the mother of death because she accepted to the offerings of death.

Hence I will forever tell everyone to know what you God is trying to tell them because man mislead and trust me death – sin infinitely kills. You will be no more.

Death cannot change hence there is two. Every creation – life must conform to X because X is in us all. It is in both male and female because originally there was on Fe – She and not He.

Yes this is why God is XY no not male. God is Female in the physical world and Male in the spiritual world. God is both Male and Female but in his purest form God is neither seen or unseen because no one can see pure energy in its truest form. No not even with your spiritual eye – eye within your Triangle.

MICHELLE

My Collective – The Dark Side of Me – Part One

God it's not about the circle being broken anymore it's about life – growth

God I don't want to grow down in evil I need to grow up in you – life

God I do not want to join evil nor do I want to die or even work for evil. I need to be with you become one in truth and honesty with you

I need us to be truly and totally devoted to your cause and that is giving humanity – everyone the full and total truth honestly.

God I need all that I do to be done for you truthfully and honestly. I need clarity and purity to be given to all – humanity

God I need the spell that evil has cast over man – humanity to be fully broken so that humanity can see what they have done to self and you

I need humanity to truly and honestly see who the devil is and what he stands for

God I need you to start preparing a place for your people. God you cannot let them get the mark of the beast. God you have to separate us your good people from evil and make us live in truth with you.

God we need our own economy
We need our own food – plants
We need our own clothing stores
Designers

We need our own television studios
Radio stations
We need our own doctors
Our own hospitals

We need our own homes
Our own grocery stores that don't sell unclean meat – pork

We need our own lawyers

We need our own
Men and women that is truthful and righteous – truly honest and faithful to you – the family

God our economy must be truthful and honest it can never lie or be dishonest nor can it be based on speculation or futures

Our food plants must be clean and void of harmful chemicals food colorings. Everything must be organic and not genetically modified

God our clothing stores and designers must be trendy up to date not explicit or elicit but the fashion and fashion designers must stay true and honest to your sexy and naughty side

God our television and radio stations cannot be explicit remember the children in our fold. These television and radio stations must be family oriented and under no circumstances be biased nor can they spread hate they must be truthful to you. They must be fun trendy play good music and not be hung up on Gospel all the time

Songs must be clean well no swearing all the time and I know I should be one to talk with what I've written in this book and my other books

God have mercy because my language is more than foul and you know it. Chalk one up for the cusser in me but God books can swear but music is different. God this time around music must not swear because in truth music is a beautiful way of communicating with you. Books are raunchy and flirty they can be fun and boring, slow but music cannot be slow or boring nor can it be raunchy. Music has to be clean because music delivers messages from you. I know I like some raunchy musical songs and yes I can name and list them but I won't because here and in this book I have set the stage for double standards and I have to say forgive me because certain things I do not have clarity on meaning I do not know so bare with me my peeps true loved ones and friends. When I have clarity I will infinitely and definitely let all of you know.

God music cannot spread hate because music soothes. It's our communication tool to others and the universe despite the different genres. God music is life because everything grows in music – yes sound and vibrations.

God our doctors and hospitals have to be clean and honest. The best interest of everyone should be their main concern. They must always strive to cure and keep the body clean and pure at all times. God they have to work with you to heal whether it is in the operating room or their own office.

I know what you are saying I did not listen and you are correct because you did give me a cure for aids and it was I that neglected your call. I was the one not to write the information down so yes right there I am guilty because I could have saved the lives of plenty and for this I am punishable because the young lady did give me the cure three (3) times in that one dream. She could not give me the cure for that which ails me and she told me this she could only give me the cure for that which ails her and I did neglect her. Yes stupidity on my part but I have to leave this alone because I did do her wrong as well as condemned a lot of people to further pain and suffering. I accept guilt and sin for this because like I said I did her wrong therefore I sinned – did wrong.

God our homes and grocery stores must be kept clean and immaculate at all times but this is a struggle for me and many that have nasty kids and no matter how much you tell them to clean they refuse to. It's as if they like to live in all things unclean.

Yes soothing music should be played at home at all times or whenever possible meaning your body – mind calls for it because good music calms and soothes the mind.

God heavy metal is too loud way too loud but to each his own if it soothes some people give them a heavy metal station to listen to as long as the music is free of chanting and talking to the devil. God we so don't want the devil coming in as a matter of fact no heavy metal it hurts the brain, invoke the dead, it is of the devil so no heavy metal music soft rock, Air Supply music like that will do. Yes I like Meat Loaf, Marianas Trench, Hedley, Nickelback and Fifi Dodson. Meatloaf's Bat out of Hell is still classic can't help it. Yes music like that will do but not the crap we are subjected to listening to.

Rap never ever – none. Can't stand today's version of it. Whatever happened to the days of Kool Moe Dee, Run DMC good rap not crap?

God don't let me get started on some of the crap that's associated with Reggae Music. God do you hear some of the artist them lately?

God give me good music like Bob Marley, Culture conscious music like Duane Stephenson, Morgan Heritage and Tarrus Riley sings. God this music will never go out of style and please do not let Duane Stephenson come out with crap or sing crap.

God Sean Paul has changed now he's singing crap that makes absolutely no sense plus he's singing with anyone and anything wow simply sickening. Now the brain is wondering if he has crossed over to the dark side.

God just give me Shaggy and continue to make him come out with good clean fun triple decker fun music that is wholesome. God I still love It wasn't me, strength of a woman, wild tonight. God let's not forget try and leave go with Alison Hinds and sweet Jamaica with Mr. Vegas and Josey Wales. God tore that up. Can't stop listening to these too songs they are timeless – classic. God with Sweet Jamaica this song makes you want to dance and go back to your true roots. God Sean Paul is not far off meaning he's not totally gone so bring him back so we can have breakfast Jamaican style. No scrap that see and know too much so scrap the breakfast Jamaican Style and please squash the Calypso by Shaggy because sey im look sey im a go Trini and mi bun dat not inna reggae style even though the 3 dads own the majority of Jamaica. Fiya fi dem dem betta noa dat. Hence hell is full of black people especially Jamaican. Dem Trini own – Dem slave owned because the Trinity own dem an dem no noa it. Dem sell you out God hence dem no own a damned thing. Yes the wanga gut and licky licky style. No wonder dem caane stop beg bread down a wafe. Yes for those who don't noa di wafe a di IMF – World Bank hence we have become Wafe Dogs – dogs without a bone and home.

Konshens big up yourself don't know why mi like you. Something strong and powerful about you. A know di power so walk good because the mind no freada no body and truss mi mi no waane touch dat dey button so mi a leave you alone but mi like you. Maybe one day mi caane meet you. No mi naa solicit yu mi waa meet you. Mi waan si if mi right about you.

God love songs like KC and JoJo, Kenny Lattimore sing gets me in the mood sometimes. Prince oh God we can't forget Prince he can bring me Diamonds and Pearls any day yes including purple rain not to mention what we can do in his little red corvette. Sorry Prince but I just had to go there. God for you by Kenny Lattimore is more than timeless because I will forever dedicate the song For You to you. It is beautiful the perfect love song so please do not let this song fade because like I said it is more than timeless. Yes I know Eric Benet sings love songs but I am so infinitely not into him. Something about him that I can't stand – do not like. Yes Maxwell is the key he will do and yes Tyrese, Tyrese, Tyrese. God he can sing to me any day, anytime, anywhere, any how because the man is finer than hot chocolate. He's my baby for keep – for real. God Tyrese knows the right way to serenade a woman and he can serenade me anyway. Yes God he is my black and delicious chocolate fix and sugar. Pow Pow damn Tyrese I have to tell your Moms thanks for making a fine piece of chocolate heaven like you. Wow you are a fine black man. Wow yes you are pow pow pow because you can sing me love songs live any day. God the man has a powerful voice did you see him live on BET. God what woman wouldn't want to jump him? Sorry sorry getting carried away. Sorry God but I have to control myself. Laugh God because you know me and my good clean fun with the finer things in life – my chocolate heavens – yes your fine and delicious black gods.

Ah yes Ms. Shirley Murdock as we lay and heavenly. Ah music to my ears. I wonder why they don't play music like these anymore in the grocery stores and in our homes instead of some of the crap we hear today. God the music I truly leave in your care because this is your baby the true voice and sound you have given to man. Some distort and some don't but I am hoping the music we choose from now on truly reflect you and the family our family.

God our lawyers cannot represent the guilty lest they too become guilty.

God when they represent the guilty they too are saying they are guilty and they would be in league with sin - the guilty. They are condoning sin and this cannot be. You cannot give sin right when sin know and knows beyond a shadow of a doubt that they are wrong – guilty.

God these lawyers must be clean. They must represent good and be good – do good at all cost. They must not make sin make them guilty. They have to secure a place with you not just for them but also for their children and the people they represent. God it's not to say they can't represent people but if a man or woman is guilty do not say they are not guilty when they are.

God I have learned the hard way and this is why I try my best to go by the truth and do all the good that I can do in truth and honesty. If I am guilty why would I want a good or bad person to represent me? Why should I let them soil themselves because of me? I have to admit guilt and shame. Is that not the right thing to do?

God life is given. Death was not given to man we accepted death and because we know the truth now we must live for life – truth and not death.

God we know criminal law is not the only avenue for them – lawyers. There is corporate or Business Law Family Law. These are other avenues as well as being judges that uphold the law. They will not be held guilty if they operated under the guidelines or laws given to them by the judicial system. They have to do their jobs honest and clean given the laws that they were given. It's not to say that if there are unfair practices within the judicial system they cannot change it. They can seek to change the unfair laws because as humans we all make mistakes commit error – wrongs including me.

MICHELLE

God I feel as if it's over today.
God I feel as if it's over now no not my life but something something is just not right.

There is a solemness as if I am waiting – my spirit is waiting for something negative to happen

God something is going to happen I feel it but what I do not know. Maybe it's just me today but yet I have a feeling that the worst is yet to come

God man cannot prepare for this. God if prayer cannot save us – man what will?

God psalms 23 mean nothing it is not true anymore. Psalms 23 cannot save man anymore. Psalms 23 cannot save man from what's to come. God what do we do?

God I know this now because time and time again you have shown me that psalms 23 cannot save man from spiritual evil. Psalms 23 cannot save us from physical wickedness –evil so the only psalms that is left is Psalms One (1). We must live by this psalms Psalms 1 and separate from evil as well as evil and wicked people.

We must not go where they go.

We must not sit with them nor eat with them

We must not commune with them nor drink with them

We must cut off all access and communication with evil – wicked and evil people

God this is going to be hard considering organizations are in league with evil. They do things that are evil including kill.

God every system of things is run by evil and I would like to say there is no getting around this but I would be incorrect – wrong. I would be downplaying you and that would be a grave injustice on my part when it comes to you.

All I can say is that we will need a totally new and different society; a society that truly loves life and themselves; a society that lives by their integrity – your truth.

We will need a banking system that is clean. A system based on you, your principles and your integrity.

God we will need doctors, lawyers, dentist, eye doctors, computer programmers no no hackers because people's privacy is sacred and we need everyone to live by your principles – integrity. These people must value life as well as put you first. They must walk in your integrity. They must truly help the people that come to them in a good way given the knowledge that they know. God they must truly work for you.

God we need pharmacists and scientists that are like this too. Everything positive and good they must do for you and your people too.

MICHELLE

God you know what I don't know what to say. I am waiting for an opening from you but yet I cannot see it.

You know what I am so not going to go there.

God tonight clearly show me what to do in my life.

In many ways I am scared not because I do not trust you but because you are not always there.

The timeline remember. Your time and my time are different – miles, even years apart. Got to leave that where it is so don't think for a minute that I don't trust you because I infinitely do.

Any ho how are you doing today?

Do you miss me?

You better say I do and yes my hand is a kimbo so you had better say I do.

Come here put your head on my shoulders. No no that won't do let me lay and you can lay your head on my chest. There there do you feel better? There let me play in your hair and make you feel better.

No talkie just you relax unwind while I turn the lights down low and play three little birds and no woman no cry by Bob Marley.

Rastararfi Is you know that. Rastafari will always be because your angels are Rasta they are for I – you and yes they will forever live because you created them this way. They are in a form that no man on the face of this planet can dispute. Just as you made me your angels are for me RASTAFARI. Just look at the true nappy hair. Long and twisted like a Rasta Man hence Rastafari represents the hair of every black man across the globe. So Rastafari I is because they do not defile the hair – yes their nappy hair.

Now Lovey close your eyes and let your stress dissipate. Calm down and cool down because you are in my true and loving arms.

There you go forget the stress the anguish of this world the earth and spiritual world.

Don't let wicked and evil people stress you.
Do not let evil and wicked spirits stress you either.

God you are with me the one that truly loves you.

Keep your eyes closed take a nap and when you awake I will be right here with you – laying with you.

MICHELLE

My Collective – The Dark Side of Me – Part One

God you can be angry with me all you want but you have to put up with me and my venting

You have to put up with my anger and yes I am going to blame you because you caused it.

I want to be like everyone now. I want to blame you for everything. I'm not lying. I want to blame you.

I want to be spoilt

Yes I am going to be a spoilt brat because I am not getting my way with you today so yes I am going to be spoilt and you can't do anything about it because I don't want you to.

I want to cuss use the f word. Tell the world f you and royally kiss my black ass.

No God it's no joke so don't you be laughing because today I am going to be spoilt. I am going to vent because I am tired. Tired of this awful life I am living.

Tired of the ill health

Tired of the pain I am feeling

Tired of not being able to do what I want when I want and yes I will say it again I am tired of you.

Yes I am venting. This is the only way I know how to and no I don't want to cheat on my man because I don't have any apart from you so no I don't want to cheat on you it's simply disgusting and makes me want to vomit. Yuk disgusting. Me cheat on you infinitely forget it because it is disgusting to me. Been there done that and I did learn my lesson so I do not walk the whoring road anymore besides I said I was venting I never said I wanted to commit sin. I never said I wanted to be a walking abomination anymore.

God how dare you let my mind suggest cheating? Now you have done it. If you want to live in sin commit sin go ahead and do it. Forget about me because the day you do I will leave your ass yes your fucking ass. Trust me you had better run and hide because I will get to you quicker than the devil if you turn become sin or even think of doing anything that is sinful or a lie.

Hell no. Hell will have no fury like my fury trust me. All that you do, all that you created will be destroyed at my hands if you ever turn to sin or even entertain the words of sin do you hear me. I've come too far, struggled too long for you to become sin. Not on my watch do you hear me.

MICHELLE

My Collective – The Dark Side of Me – Part One

No one knows the importance of a name
No one knows God no one knows

The name that is given is important
The name of the land you are born in is vital

Many lands house deceit but none know the importance of the land they were born in

Everyone is living in vain
They live to destroy
Live to kill

All that is important they have forgotten
They truly do not know

God I know the importance of a name especially the name of the land I was born in

Many do not know but I know therefore I live in my little world void of evil but it does not mean it's totally void because I have children and they too exhibit evil. They have their friends and they too exhibit evil – they refuse to learn.

Life is not the same when you live amongst evil. In many ways you don't want to be amongst them. Reside near them – reside with them.

MICHELLE

There is goodness in the darkness
There is goodness around me

All that I do I do the good that I can when I can
I do not store my goodness up in man but in God

In all that I do I do not seek favor from man I seek favor from God. I seek truth true love because I know if God does not answer me he too will become wrong. So I do not seek anything in man all I seek I seek in God.

God fails but God can never fail
Man cannot bless you only God can
Man cannot give life he can only take it away – by the sinful and wicked things that we do – his sinful and wicked ways

God is the one to give life and he did give all of us life but we are the ones to destroy life. We alter self even try to alter our genes but no man can alter the genes because the genes is hence Genesis – the beginning.

Man have become the true destroyers
The true devils because evil is born
Evil kills and men has and have killed in the name of their evil and deceitful gods
Some live to kill
We all destroy
We cannot learn because all we see is sin – control hence we seek and destroy like it's a video game.

MICHELLE

God let your city reign
God let the temples of evil be blown down
Be utterly destroyed never to return on land or in heaven again

Let evil return unto evil
God return the plots, blows and schemes of evil back to sender – back to evil

God I know billionaires are going to lose it all because all they live for is vanity – greed

God wow all around is greed. Man has it but cannot truly stretch forth and give to the poor.

The rich man has it but refuse to give in your name – in the name of you

God I am amazed at the wealth of man but yet the heart is dark do not truly give or know how to give. All they do is accumulate and accumulate while the poor in their countries go unfed – kill to eat.

God I know they are going to lose it all because all that they have and do none store it up in you

God I can feel it. I know this but yet helpless to help. God many billionaires are going to lose it all.

Many are going to become paupers – die

God from my dream it's going to start with Russia one particular billionaire in Russia but God I am not sure because sometimes our dreams do not walk or talk straight. These billionaires are going to be the first to lose it all because vanity is their stay. Greed is their way and stay. Everything that they do they do it in vain – for vanity. Vanity consumes them. It is their calling so woe be unto them because they do love vain things – love in vain.

God strength is there but what is the point in having strength when all that you say and do is for vanity and not the good of the people or the good that you do.

God gold and copper – steel will topple the world's economy and everything will for a surety crumble.

God gold will have no value. It will be thrown away like garbage. It will become worthless. Gold is not valued in the spiritual realm it's garbage but yet man put value on this yes in gold.

It's not power. It is a foolish man that thinks gold is power. He will live for naught and when he finds out he will know that his gold is nothing but fool yes fool's gold. It is worth nothing.

God this global collapse is real but yet the rich cannot comprehend this so they continue to live in vain. They continue to over produce. They continue to kill all in vain.

God – Lovey ooh what a day when the super rich becomes paupers – losers in their own game of sin

Yes they will die and be reduced to rubble. They will truly have nothing and they will find out the bitter way the cost of vanity – living vain - greed.

MICHELLE

God the global meltdown is pending. It is inevitable there will be no more billionaires – millionaires that will call this land home because it they will be gone – no more

All that man has stored up in the devil will be reduced to rubble. They will have none because everything will crumble

God I feel it in the pit of my stomach. It's only a matter of when yes a matter of time. Lovey thank you for not letting me store up anything in man because all that I have, all that is given to me I store it all in you because I know you can never be wrong. You can never – infinitely never fail me

Lovey man can change their ways but they will refuse to so therefore they will be reduced to rubble they will crumble. God before the global meltdown starts please prepare a good place for your people. Prepare a true home for them and me.

God it is going to get vile more vile and bad – wickeder than it is now, so before things start to happen let your people flee from the lands of the devil – evil. Let the exodus start God because life will not be pretty. Man will live like scavengers – cannibals upon the land. Soon there will be no food to eat – global warming.

God please I am pleading with you secure a place for your people in the mother land if you have to. God please you have to secure your people and not make them go down in sin.

God this global depression wow will be so bad that many will run to you when it's too late. God you have to nag your people and show them the truth like you have shown me.

God you cannot let us get caught up in the mess of sin. You cannot close the door on us because the full truth is not yet known. You have to give us the full truth.

It's not going to be pretty for humanity but from our way of living it seems like this is what humanity wants. God the super rich wants this so we alter your teaching and self to please our vain ways – greedy self.

God and Lovey for me do not let this global depression and recession hurt me or your people.

Do not let it touch us or touch my family. God protect your people the ones that truly love you and do things to please you. And God this includes my peeps true loved ones and friends. You cannot forget them God because they do support you and do all they can for you.

God I will forever bug you until you get fed up of me. Protect your people and bring them to the place that they need to be. I will repeat myself over and over again. You cannot allow your people to go down with sin and his people in hell.

God you have to protect them and their economy. God separate the good from the bad meaning separate good from evil and let us have our enterprise and economy including banks in you. God quickly help us so that when this evil system fails we have a good clean and cherished system in you.

MICHELLE

My Collective – The Dark Side of Me – Part One

People I have to add this in this book because this bitch in the spiritual realm is pissing me off.

Yes she's an older woman – an elder to me meaning she is like a mother figure in the grandmother stage but from time to time she's appeared to me and I am so getting fed up of her because she wants me to come her way. I refuse her but yet she is there and I so want to shut her down permanently so that she does not bother me anymore.

She makes me so angry because she comes to me with religion and I am not about religion. I see her as my enemy because I think she wants me to fail God and I refuse to fail God. And in all that we do I will tell all of you to be mindful of the spiritual because certain forces do give the living power and if they fail in the physical they will pull out all the stops in the spiritual for you to fail.

There's a greater pull in the spiritual world. It's like when you meet this person and that attraction is so great that you feel this force pulling you towards that person. It is that strong and if you are not careful you end up doing something real stupid. It's a force like this I am talking about. Sometimes that force does not have to pull. Sometimes it leads your spirit. Maybe I do not understand or comprehend what this woman is trying to do but with her I will indefinitely have my guard up when it comes to her.

Trust me I got so pissed off that I took my frustrations out on God and this is what I told him.

See below>>>next page>>>>>>>>>
God what the hell part of no evil around me do you not get?

God the earth is riddled with garbage on the land.

Seen the trash and now the Christians are complaining that it's too much to clean.

The Spanish are complaining about the mess too but we created the mess God. We dirtied the water. We caused spiders to build webs so we cannot get to you.

We polluted the land. This lady God in the spiritual world that is causing me grief – strife shut her down now because in this vision I went to church – one foot went in the door and I said I've betrayed God because I went on church grounds by mistake.

Got let me tell you something I refuse to lay with a married and dirty man to pollute myself. And God secure my daughter in the home that she is in because hell will have no fury when it comes to me and anyone hurting her. She's our child despite her ways to me. I cannot give up on her so please secure her and her virginity because if you don't I give you my word that you God will have hell to pay when it comes to my daughter so you had better secure her good and right in your fold.

God after this dream – vision I have to get serious and wicked with you because life is the key to everything and if you make dirty men or woman devour her I swear you will have hell to pay because I am trusting you to secure and protect all my children in a good way. I do not joke when it comes to my children you know that so please secure them in the physical and spiritual world.

As for the church in my vision God know that I will never betray you so no matter what this bitch do to me in the spiritual for me to betray you it's not going to work because I am living and she is dead.

God stop playing with me. Stop playing with me, stop playing with me because you know not the extent of my true love for thee so stop because I am not messing with you and this bitch is getting to me.

I am tired of her fucking around with me in the spiritual realm – world and I am bent. I am mad God. Trust me I am bent because this, this whoring Delilah will not leave me alone and you refuse to shut this bitch down and you refuse to shut her up.

What the fuck part of no evil whether living or dead, spirit or foe do you not comprehend God. No God I'm sorry for swearing but I am bent and I need to vent so I am coming to you with all that I have.

I need my life with you to be good and clean in the spiritual world and she is taking my glory and life from me. Also, if the spiritual world is not clean how the hell am I going to be with you?

Tell me because I am yelling – my spirit is yelling.

God get it through your head that I loathe all evil. I despise evil because evil is taking away my happiness with you all around. I need a clean place with you in the spiritual realm also and evil is pulling out all the stops in the spiritual world for me to deceive and fail you.

God I refuse to go to sins churches but this bitch won't stop because she is testing my faith, trying my patience and the next time she does this I will illuminate her by any means necessary. No I will not soil my hands but if there is a way to lock her infinitely in hell and let death deal with her I will. I am tired of her because I have my new cleaning tool to clean up the earth so you had better let me use it in a good and positive way. You had better let no one steal it or take my cleaning tool away from me because though the land is polluted with paper – garbage it was not hard for me to clean. The garbage on the land is clear like unto clear cheese wrapping paper – wrapping paper like they use to wrap sliced cheese.

But God I will not let this bitch interfere with me and you because I told you I need and want to cleave to you in a good way for all eternity – indefinitely and this bitch of a demon oman cum tek yu wey from mi. Afta mi try so hard to stay on track wid you this raase clate stench of a whoring drangcrow wey stink wus dan ded daage – this piece of shit that nobody wants a cum interfere with my peace and tranquility with you. She wants me to fail you in the spiritual world. God shi really a bark up the wrong tree because I will literally beat her ass slap bak to hell. I am the wrong bitch she wants to fuck with when it comes to you God. So God you are forewarned in the harshest of ways because I do not dick around when it comes to my relationship with you. No I am serious. No one comes between us so you had better shut down this bitch all spiritual evil and wickedness infinitely as well as eternally indefinitely.

This is no fucking joke. I am dead serious. My relationship with you is serious – cherished and absolutely no one should interfere with me and you. I don't care who it is do not disrespect my space with you and this woman is doing it – disrespecting my space with you. She's trying my patience and when she does this you God will feel my wrath – anger because I am trusting you to protect and defend me. I am trusting you to shield me from all demons everywhere and if you can't do this then what the hell good are you to me? If I can't trust you God then who can I trust?

No I do not trouble sin so sin should not trouble me. I did not go into this woman's abode and provoke her so she should not come into my abode – space with you and provoke me. This earth does not belong to her because she does not have the balls to create a universe for herself and her nasty people so don't come into my domain and space with you with her bullshit. I don't need it and you know this God.

No bitch must come or should come and disrespect me or you. No flatly NOOOOO and you know this. This titan belongs to Good – belongs to You – belongs to Good Life and dis dutty stinking crebby crebby way har pussy stink wussa dan ten day tunda a cum fuck wid my relationship with you. God you want di whole world tun upside dung with my blood clate fury. No you no noa mi when it comes to you. Mi a di wrong bitch this Jezebel of a locust want come fuck wid. Truss mi I will go into hell and beat the fuck out of her and tun up the atomic heat on her. I will literally throw more shit on her so you had better warn her and shut her down because she don't want me to do it because truss mi God mi temper is hotter, infinitely hotter than yours. Fi mi tempa hotta than death's sting so tell lef mi alone. Mi a raw baane Jamaican you don't fuck wid us and wi man – inna my case my God. Mi a di wuss blood clate terror when it comes to you – the one I infinitely truly love. Death has nothing on mi because death fraide a mi when mi done with har because mi wi mek death shit im pants when mi done so tell dis dutty stinky frought of germs mine who she a trouble.

Mi naa trouble har so shi no fi trouble mi and yu. You're my God and mi a no like di ada messengers dem. Mi a Lyons – a fucking she lion that protects her loved ones and truss mi I will do it at all cost. I know what I have in you God and no one should come and destroy me to get to you. No one should come and destroy me and you or the relationship I have with you.

So you are forewarned. Shut spiritual evil down because my mouth can get nastier and filthier than this and truss mi yu no want mi fi cuss yu because you will get it worse than her. You don't want me turning against you or loathing you and you know this so I suggest you keep this bitch in her place and at bay. Lock her away as well as lock her people away. You don't want me cussing you. Truly you don't because mi head hotter than hot when you rub me the wrong way.

I infinitely truly love you.
Infinitely truly care about you.
Infinitely truly cherish you and the relationship that we have so please shut every spiritual evil down when it comes to me and my family and the good seeds you have given me. And God my family had better be good or else.

God evil have and has no right trying to get me to deceive you. Evil has and have no right trying to break my bond with you.

God why the fuck don't she go find her blood clate cesspool of a degenerate husband. Shi no have nottun fi du ada dan crass mi spirit in a di early maaning. A who shi.

Shi no si no man no want har. Shi rev out like bruk dung bus.

Yu no si shi caane fix

No mi mad now. No spare part or new part no want har bloodclate an a mi shi have time fa. Ole aan God yu no tell evil bout mi. Yu no tell dem no fi mess with mi. A beating yu want to God. No no laugh. No yu really want mi fi get mada an tek di guava stick to yu.

Don't mess wid mi because yu caane truly love like mi. No don't smile or laugh. What is mine is mine and you're mine mine mine mine do you hear me so no ded daag nufi cum trouble mi and mi honey which is you because you are sweet.

No God evil is evil and evil stinks. You're my God, My Boo, My Lovey, My Millie Mango, My Jackfruit, My Flower, My Everything – ALL, so no one don't mess with me and you or should mess with me and you.

God it is wrong and unjust for evil – spiritual wickedness to want me to betray you or cause you pain in the spiritual and physical world. This is wrong and you know it.

I will not dirty the spiritual world or the physical world for them because all evil must die a harsh and painful death so you had better shut her up and indefinitely shut her down. You God is my right and no spiritual demon has that right to try to take you from me or me from you. This is wrong and sinful and you need to shut evil down because of this. You must shut all physical and spiritual evil down because they are blatantly interfering between me and you hence they are breaking the laws of creation – the Ying and Yang in both worlds. Yes sin is sin – wrong is wrong but if I do not accept sin – Will then why is sin bothering me. Why is sin interfering with me? This is automatic death God and you know this. I am not interfering with sin because my books are not for sin but for your good and righteous people. Sin knows his domain and the domain of sin is not mine because I have given myself over to life, honest and truth – true love and that truth and true love is you.

No sin cannot say I am living in his world because this world was not created by sin and although I live in the North you know God know how I feel about this and this is why I petition you truthfully for your home – our clean and good home here on earth as well as in the spiritual realm. You God cannot aide death in destroying your own. This is infinitely wrong and sinful on your part. You are allowing evil to win and this cannot be because I told you I do not choose Bad I choose Good – You and if you let me go down with evil I am taking you down with me because I am glued to You – Your Goodness.

Evil must pay – this woman must pay for her sins God. For what she did to me she must be held accountable for disrespecting me and you. I will not stand for it God because your laws are clear, right and exact and no one should willingly try to let me break them. I am trying to live good and right by your laws and it is wrong for spiritual evil to taunt me in anyway.

I do not taunt evil nor do I go in the way of spiritual or physical evil so evil have no right to taunt me or even trying to get me to break my word and vow to you.

God this is not the first time this woman is doing this to me and I refuse her entry in my life so why do you keep letting this happen to me. No church on the face of this planet is clean. They are all filthy – dirty and I do not want anything to do with them because they tell abominable lies on you and this is infinitely wrong and sinful. As for my books God the journey and journey's I take in the physical world for them (my books – our books) I ask that you open good and positive doors for me. Yes I will walk in the valley of the shadow of death with them but I cannot fear evil anymore because you are my right and left hand. You are my eyes and ears. You are my shield that surround me all the time. You are my protector and stay all the time. Because I do not know the roads to travel I come to you for help and guidance in a true, good and honest way. Yes I see the precipits before me but I am trusting you not to make me fall in them or be overcome or surrounded by them.
I do not need evil leading me in anyway God and I've told you this. I've told you you are all I need God so why are you allowing evil in our domain – our space? Come on now. I do not send evil to you so why are you allowing this to happen to me?

How can I swell with you in the spiritual world if that domain is not clean?

What part of Goodness and cleanliness do you not get God?

What part of infinitely no evil around me or surround me nowhere – anywhere do you not get God? I was not born into this world to be a slave or a victim to evil anywhere and this goes for the spiritual domain as well so why are you continuously letting sin – evil get to me? Clean is clean and good is good. Truth is truth and cannot change so clean up the mess and filth in the spiritual realm – world because trust me you do not want or need me to hold you accountable for sin and filth in the spiritual world as well. I am no nonsense and no joke when it comes to you and me – our relationship because our relationship is truly valued above anything else. Our relationship is honest and truthful and I cannot lose it – the relationship we have because of an evil she demon. God your anger cannot compare to mine because my anger is more vicious that yours you know this.

What is mine is mine like I've said and no dry branch must interfere because I will light the fire hotta dan hell and burn her there. Hell's spiritual fire does not compare to mine when it comes to you because like I've told you I am the one to literally pick you up and put you to the side and say baby I've got you – I've got this and lay it into the person or persons that try to take you from me. Hell hath nothing not one thing that I want or need so no one in hell should interfere with me. Hell is cut off – locked off from me and my children, my family and the good seeds you have given me God.

Don't fuck with me and you because I am that crass and deadly when I am angry in regards to you so tell this piece of shit to stop messing with me because I am the wrong Jamaican she's fucking with.

I told you I will defend you. I do not provoke anyone and she should stop provoking me. I am not patient like you God hence I tell you everything. I come to you with my anger and what's upsetting me. The relationship I have with you is mine hence I swear at you because this is the way I feel. This is my way of venting and you know and understand this. Like I said I value you because it is you that I can cleave to hence I will tell others not to do what I do with you unless they have a true and honest relationship with you.

This woman – female demon gave herself over to death. I gave myself over to true, honest and good life – You and not because I am in her stinking domain – the North should she bother me. Evil did not create the world you did God so evil should not be in this world or anywhere for that matter. And God this I blame you for because I am a Southerner not a Northerner. Southerners do not like to fight. We enjoy and value life – peace and tranquility – harmony. Southerners should not mel or gel with Northerners because the North is the center of all evil. The North is the land of sin and evil. The North is the birthplace of sin. This you know but yet you insist on keeping me prisoner in the North – Sin.

You insist on keeping me here when you know it is infinitely wrong.

The North has nothing to do with the South because the North is Aries land – warring kingdoms where as the South is the lands of peace – truth hence the South infinitely has nothing to do with the North.

We don't want to marry the North or have anything to do with their people or land and by you keeping your people in the North you are infinitely wrong. Yes this is why the North has all the say over you and your people because we are living in lands not known to us meaning we are living in sin as sin was never known to us because we were created good. We are sins prisoners and we have to break free from sin.

Yes people and this is in part why sin said and low man has become like one of us knowing good and evil. We became like evil and we started to partake of evil. This is why evil is in the physical and spiritual world as well as in all humans.

I have asked you time and time again to shut down evil everywhere both in the physical and spiritual and you are ignoring me.
I am not going against Will God because Will is good and evil. I have made the right choice for me and my children – family as well as the good seeds you have given me. I cannot choice for evil and wicked people. And God when it comes to my family and children the choice goes for the good ones not the wicked ones and if you ever let any of my children be wicked or participate in any evil woe be unto to you because I did choose life – goodness for all of them. No I did not do this at birth because I did not know and now that I know I am doing it making the good decision for them. I am making the right decision for them because they did come from my loins. Forget it GOODNESS all that is good must come from their loins and their children's loins for infinite generations – indefinitely. No evil must come from any of them do you hear me God. You have my word that if any of my children or their offspring participate in any form of evil your abode will mash up because of me. I will not tolerate sin or have any more sin in my family. This is our family God and you need to respect my wishes and desires of goodness also. No come on now. I cannot be truly loving you and my children are evil – participate in evil. Come on now what sense does that make. Hell no honey my children and future generations must indefinitely and infinitely clingy and good to you honey. No loopholes so if there is any I suggest you

erase them and close all gaps everywhere to evil and wicked people.

God spiritual evil is pissing me off and if it continues I give you my word that I will piss you off and hold you infinitely accountable for sin and treason. Yes hold you infinitely accountable for failing me all around. You know me God and I told you I am no joke. I am no nonsense when it comes to me and you. No one has a right to trouble what's mine. No one not even you. Well you can but you know what I mean. Our space is our space and it should not be polluted by evil anywhere. No come on now.

A no mi mek this dry branch no have life come on now.

A no mi mek Satan – Sin rev har out so dat shi no have did right man.

A no mi mek har caane come to you for life. A she dutty har self so wey shi a interfere wid mi fa. Mi tell har sey mi like or love dutty. A caane tan di smell of stink so wey shi a badda mi fa.

Mi wane yu God an yu naa heed mi waaning dem. Mi a waane yu again. If yu mek dis dutty Jaysi wata, crebby crebby drangcrow cum between me and you yu had better create a different universe for me where I cannot find you because your world will tun up. Mash up wus dan Tsunami mash up lan and life. You are duly warned.

I will not have anyone using me to get to you. I refuse them and will refuse you if this continues in the spiritual realm – world. I've cut off evil in the physical so no physical wickedness better not try. God you have land locked already – yes the destruction of man and you must lock down the spiritual world and its evils. You cannot give physical evil a place to flee in the spiritual world because spiritual thwarting is deadlier than physical thwarting.

I will not tolerate interference from no one when it comes to you. I've been through too much hell on earth for spiritual evil to come and add their crap to my map. I will not have it because like I've said and will forever say I will pick you up and put you to the side and rib it into evil. I will destroy evil because my mouth no have kina when it comes to defending you.

Mi a waane yu. Waane evil – spiritual evil – this bitch because she's rubbing me the wrong way and interfering in my life with you. I will not betray you like she did. I infinitely refuse to. I did not accept evil and his offerings and you know this infinitely God. I did not accept evils offerings. I accepted good, true and honest life and from I did this evil has violated my decision to good, true and honest life with their taunting of my spirit and for this judgment must be infinitely and indefinitely be served in the physical and spiritual realm – world.

This act is a blatant violation of my life – privacy. This is not the first time this woman is doing this. She's been trying to get me to violate our agreement of truth and I refuse her entry. I refuse to go into her dirty domain – churches.

My decision is final God. My agreement with you is final and absolute in both worlds – the physical and spiritual. She must as well as sin and death must live with the decision I made of living a good, truthful and honest life with you. I did not choose evil I chose good life – you. She cannot cohorse me into breaking my truth – good truth and honest bond – word with you. She is wrong and she will fail. I did not accept Satan so why the hell would I accept her?
She has nothing to offer me that I need and want and even if she did I do not need and want it God because I

infinitely and indefinitely have you so please let her indefinitely flee. Lock her away indefinitely. She is not a part of my world nor is she a part of your world God so do not have her coming around me anymore. I don't care if she's black either because not all blacks are a part of your world. Many belong to the devil's kingdom hence hell is full of black people. She accepted death so let her live with death because none in the physical know that the wickedest death a man can have is spiritual death. This death is so painful and long that many will want to turn to you God and can't because the decision they make in the physical binds and bound them in the spiritual. You cannot interfere with their decision hence Noah's ark is almost gone because many have chosen religion and in your kingdom – world there are no religions. None can understand the concept – story of Noah. None was saved because all have chosen religion over you hence when the door to your ark was closed none was saved except for Noah and his family. And in all truth Noah's Ark was not then it is now – this day and time – the here and now.

I accepted life and it is with life – good life that I will stay indefinitely and infinitely true to. I will infinitely not betray you for her or anyone because I know the goodness in life. As humans we do not care because we are selfish. All we see are our selfish needs and I refuse to be like them – humanity.

God maybe you want to betray me and stand against me but I will never betray you or stand against you for anyone not even my children and family. I know what you took me out of and because of your goodness to me I truly thank you and cling to you. My word is my word. It is faithful and true. If you want to go God go but you will never, infinitely never find or have another child that infinitely loves you as much as me. Yes I know I could be wrong but given the people – humanity in this world I stand by my word because remember anyone can say they love you but not everyone can say that they truly love you.

You and I know that the greatest gift a man or woman can have is true love – truth – you.

Love is for the devil because it is only wicked and evil people love. Meaning they hurt, lie, cheat and deceive then turn around and say they love you. Love is evol – evil. Yes love lives but true love is infinite – forever. It cannot die it can only grow into true and infinite beauty. So when a man tell me the greatest gift you can have is love I will tell them to royally kiss my MF ass. Bun dat because he's a liar and deceiver. Do not tell me about love tell me about truth – true love. So God if you lose me you will lose everything and you would have made evil win. You would be the one to be blamed for this and not me or man because you had true love and you let it go. You did not want or need good for you.

You were the one to be wrong and not me. Also for that piece of junju that classed me in my dream you tell im sey mi noa let me bold, highlight and underline. Yes I know I am writing on paper but all is bold, underline and highlighted in my head. Tell that piece of Junju say:

<u>MI NOA WHO MY FATHER IS AN IM FI GO FINE FI IM BECAUSE SEY FI MI MADDA NEVA RUN STREET LIKE BUS AND CAR. FI MI MADDA NO HAVE MILEAGE LIKE AIRPLANE SO IM FI GO CHECK FI IM AN NOA BOUT HAR. FI MI MADDA NEVA PASS ROUNE FROM HAN TO HAN LIKE HAN CART. A NO FI MI MADDA TUN SHEET PAN BED AND REV OUT LIKE MACK TRUK,CAARE, BUS, BOAT AND AIRPLANE SO IM FI WATCH WHO IM A CLASS BECAUSE SEY MI AVE MI PUPPA NAME AND IM FI GO FINE FI IM PUPPA NAME BECAUSE A LYONS MI NAME AND NO ONE CAN TAKE IT FROM ME. I WAS BORN</u>

UNDER YOUR BANNER – THE BANNER OF GOD IN THE SOUTHERN MONTH – STATE HENCE I AM A SOUTHERN BELLE – BELL. TRUST ME I WILL RING IS BELL WITH MY MOUTH BECAUSE I AM THE ONE TO CALL HUMANITY TO THE TRUTH – THE TRUTH OF GOD – YOU GOD THE TRUE AND LIVING GOD.

God how dare this piece of drangcrow shit. No drangcrow shit smell betta dan im. Im noa me but yet im a cum class and judge me. No God I am fed up of my people – black people in the spiritual realm a cum tek libaty like mi an dem a fren. Ku pan dem to. Wus dan dry bone to BC. Dem ave right? Dem a wha? Yu no si Satan ave dem unda lok an key and dem caane cum out and a mi dem ave time fa. Man check yuself because yu done wreck aredey. Don't trouble mi. Man yu stinka dan Satan shit to BC. Go fine yuself because all mi afi do a look pan a piece a shit an sey aaah a you.

Don't wrenk wid mi because im should noa betta.

Don't trouble mi because sey mi naaa trouble yu.

No God who is he to class me. He doesn't know me. I don't know him nor do I want to know him. I do not want or need to know evil nor do I want or need to know evil spirits. Evils domain is evils domain. Yes I maybe living in the North but God this is your fault. I blame you because I did not want to come here in the first place. I was taken from my homeland against my will and because of this me being in the North evil has a say over me and this is wrong. You are wrong also for this. Letting evil have a say over me and you. This is not right so because of this you are wrong. Evil made us wrong and evil has the say over me and you. Because of this evil can charge the both of us for interference and sin because we are in his land and for this we are both wrong.

Because I reside in the North evil has all rights over me and you.

We are both wrong because we are in the land of evil hence evil has all rights and right to torment us and hold us guilty of sin.

God this is why there is no peace and will be no peace. Your people must come out of the lands of the wicked. Evil does not want us in their lands so why are we going into their land. I don't want or need to be in evils land or lands so truly help your people to get out of them – their lands. God tell me something how can we live as Psalms One (1) when we are living in evil lands? Come on now. Tell me how we can be clean if we are living in dirty lands and marrying dirty people. Come on now.

How can I speak the truth and live by the truth if I am in a dirty land? Come on now. Am I not dirty? Am I not like the wicked ones because I am in their land? So how can I live true, be true if I am living in a dirty land? Come on now. Am I not making you filthy and dirty God? Come on now. Right is right and truth is truth and I am giving you the truth God. You can either hate me or truly love me. I am wrong and you are wrong because I am in a dirty land and no matter how I tell you that I don't want or need to be here you are keeping me captive against my will. I want out of this land because I don't like it. It's too cold and there's nothing for me here. You know my true feelings but yet you refuse to help me to truly and honestly clean up my homeland so that I can go back and live in peace and truth – harmony with you. No God for this keeping me here against my will I truly don't want to forgive you. I want to hold it against you. You didn't keep Moses so long in Egypt well you did so I shouldn't complain but God I truly don't want or need to be here so I complain. I know you know what's right for me but God does it have to be so long. No for real God. Couldn't you shorten my stay in this forsaken land – the land of the North – Cold – yes North Pole. God I am in the true North and trust me I infinitely so don't want to be here.

Yes God I know what's ours is ours and I have to be in hell in order to take your people out but God if your people don't want to come out what can I do? My books are in limbo even though I correct them and it has taken me years to correct them because your time is not man's time.

God not matter what is ours we have no right being in the land of sin. We are guilty of sin.

Your people – our people must separate from sin and move out of the lands of sin in a good and positive way. Yes sin must leave out – move out of our lands in a good and positive way.

We must indefinitely separate from sin. This is the only way so that when true death comes it takes its own.

God you cannot dispute this or say anything because this is the right way because it was ordained so. I need not remind you that the wages of sin is death. I am infinitely correct and right now sin can hold you accountable for sin because I am in their land – domain. I am in North America. God the North is the devil's domain and we have no right being in it. There is no justification for this. Yes our forefathers and parents took us out of our land but God that is no excuse when we have our own. Why should we suffer at the hands of evil? Why should we continue to build evil and destroy our own? What sense does that make. Don't even say my books because I did try with my own and they were the ones to refuse me but I am not giving up because one day one day I must find the right accord. That true and honest publishing company that will put you first and put my works – books on high accord. Yes I want to give up but

I have family members telling me I can't give up – well my brother anyway so I have to listen because he is wise despite the miles apart.

God we have no right in evils domain hence your people are slaves to sin. We have to give our all to sin and this is not right it is infinitely wrong. We cannot bask in the delicacies of sin and say it is of you. This is wrong and sinful on our part.

We cannot continue to build the lands of sin and say it is of you – good when we know it is not good it is wrong. We cannot live in the devil's domains and say we are going to see you this is wrong because we will never see you living in sinful and evil lands.

God no unclean spirit or human can or will enter your abode hence it is a few that is deemed to make it. Hell is full of black people remember, and if we continue to live for sin we will all fail you including me because we are living in sinful domains.

From we are living in the devil's domain nothing that we do in the name of good will be or can be good – clean.

If we are living in a dirty land we of ourselves cannot become clean. We will forever be dirty hence we will not see you God. We can only see death and become dead – slaves.

God you have to right this wrong. You cannot let us live like this because you too will become wrong – sinful – dirty.

God it's not only about me. It's about your people too.

We are living amongst evil hence evil kill us and this their right because *"the wages of sin is death."* Death is the payment of sin and none of us can hold sin guilty for this because sin did tell us the truth that his payment is death. So if you go into sins world and have children in his world you must be his slave – you must die.

We are the ones to go into the world of sin hence I comprehend Genesis and the name Jew on a different level – a true scale.

If we don't go into evils domain evil cannot hurt us or kill us hence God I need to be out of sins world – domain. I need to take my children out because I did dedicate them to good and true life – You. I need to take Life out of evils domain and carry into your good land so that they – your good people – our good people can life a clean and decent life – a truthful and good life indefinitely and infinitely. We are wrong because we are the ones to cross over into sins land – domain. We are wrong God and because we are wrong we have made you wrong. We deceived you. Yes this black lady goes beyond this because I now know why she came to me. I comprehend hence I will try my best to not travel that evil road. I know evil distort the truth but one day God one day evil will be driven out of all the domains of this land – earth.

Michelle

My Collective – The Dark Side of Me – Part One

God evil dominate and control and you continue to let it. Evil is now airborne
We cannot control it – eliminate it

Cancer dominate
Infest the body
Kills at the body at will

This is because of evils people
Men and women who design and create weapons – diseases to kill – infiltrate

Humanity has gone too far with their sins now total destruction looms. Yes economic collapse – global meltdown.

The heat comes – fire and brimstone because all that will be left on earth is dirt to eat – human flesh to devour

This is the scorpion kings – scorpions of revelations
A new form of cannibalism – the devouring of other humans – your own

This we caused on self because soon there will be no glaciers to protect man from his final doom. No one will be safe because in all we do we live to die hence we die a nasty death both in the physical and spiritual world – realm.

No one can cry or run now because the destruction of man comes now. It is before 2032. This is confirmed and now it's woe be unto man.

What have we done has come and done. The death of man has been mandated and sin – evil all evil man and woman including child must die. It is ordained and it is now so.

Michelle

God man will eat the flesh of humans more and more now. Flesh eating diseases will be on the increase. It will become the new cancer of man outnumbering the cases of AIDS and HIV.

It will be the norm because now they will tell you they have the cures for all the cancers and diseases of men. Diseases they created to kill man – humanity. Did they not know they could not or can run from the scorpion kings. The eating of the flesh – the true death of man.

All that they did could have been undone but now it's too late because the time extension of man is truly done. Man cannot extend their time on earth because 2132 was taken from men – all evil domains.

Many will cry but it is pointless because the Mountain did come time and time again but they refused. Instead they followed after prophets – wicked and evil men.

They distort the truth without knowing. They accepted wicked Sciences in their domain now man believe in secret societies and follow after them. They are like unto fools because none know the significance of the eye in the triangle. None know the significance and importance of BABY BLUE NOT BLUE IVY. Ivy is poison of the devils domain hence your people will not and cannot be fooled by the devil and his evil children – evil clans. These wretched demons can distort and say but none know you took out BABY BLUE OUT OF EGYPT LONG AGO hence the Nile will always be light blue and infinitely not dark blue – bleu.
Ah how man want to know and can never know because light blue does not signify life on earth but life with you – You God. Light Blue is the traveler's anthem for good spirits hence the devil try to use it but truly do not know.

The waterways of man of man is being destroyed. Rivers and Seas will become permanently blood red. Nothing will be left for evil men because we did – they did all to destroy the environment.

Soon there will be no more clean drinking water supply because the waterways are depleting – receding.

Ah yes God the heat comes and min will die a horrible death. Corporations will sink because many stink – greed. They too will cry – cry louder and ask where has my money gone? This is when they will find out never trust the devil and play his dirty little games.

God many use evil to kill – stay afloat but it matters not anymore because they too are going to die. None realize that evil must repay them. Evil must kill now evil is airborne. Many is looking to the future but God truly and truth be known there is no future for them in this evil domain because they must get paid for all the evils they have done. Evil will devour them because they are evils people and the 'WAGES OF SIN IS DEATH," just in case they did not know. Evil must die for their sins – abominations because all they did they did in the name of sin for sin.

Michelle

God evil is airborne no wonder we are going mad
Evil has taken to destroying the head – brain of humans

God the air and water is impure. No natural balance just death everywhere.

God doom and gloom looms but governments, scientists refuse to tell people – humanity the real and true truth.

Yes God for many its death for death and death before dishonor. But God aren't we dishonored? When we kill; when we sin; when we take a life; when we lie do we not dishonor? So why death before dishonor when we have no honor – we are all going to die?

God all evil must die hence the continuum – continuation of life – no evil must form – hath life – good life.

God it's going to take hundreds if not thousands of years to undo what evil has done to earth but God it's truly up to you because in all that evil does evil seek to kill and does kill hence the destruction of man on this planet we call earth.

God also in all that you do do not make it hard for your people. In the good lands that they reside in let the grass stay green, fruits grow and the water stay infinitely clean and abundant. But God in these lands no evil must go indefinitely hence immigration of any sort is not allowed. Not even in marriage is it allowed. Make it forbidden so no evil can come in and pollute our clean land and decent homes.

Michelle

God today I truly do not pity man – humanity because we got what we deserve

In all that we do we seek to kill and destroy and we do kill and destroy

We justify death when we know we are wrong

We justify our lies when we know we are wrong

We've made earth a killing field the justify ourselves by saying in the interest of national security, in the interest of God. We lie to justify our wrongs – sins

In all we do we lie to justify our sinful self and despite knowing this doing this we claim our lies are the truth hence we sue and go to court

The courts justify lies hence the justice system is not fair because liars and thieves are not punished equally – fairly. Murders and rapists are not punished equally – fairly. We house these people in prisons and give them just like everyone else. They have it easy hence they don't eat with their hands and sleep on the cold floor. We give them a home instead of letting them work for their daily bread.

We give them TV's to watch, books to read so that they can come out and deceive – kill some more.

We give them hot water to bathe instead of giving them cold water

We give them rights when they should have none

We pay their lawyer fees hence Legal Aide.

We cater to them hence the legal and justice system is not for good but for evil – wicked and evil people. This is evils system because in evils system criminals have all the right. This is their entitlement because we give it to them when they have none. They don't have to work for anything because all is free – we give it to them.

We burden our system for them hence humanity will never learn we will forever sin.

Ah yes God man has and have forgotten no lie can be the truth and no truth can justify lies meaning truth cannot justify lies. Truth have to be true it cannot lie.

Lies are sinful – death hence we live to lie, we lie to die hence we die – do die.

Lies lead to death hence we die in both worlds but man refuse to know and learn that the wickedest death a man – spirit can face is spiritual death – the death of the spirit.

In all that the spirit show us and tell us we refuse to listen

When we stub our toes it is the spirit that feels pain.

When we cry it's the spirit that cries

When we feel hurt it is the spirit that hurts but yet man – humanity does not know this they think its flesh.

Michelle

God the head, the head, the head

No one knows that the triangle is a window to the soul hence the eye in the triangle

God no one knows the circle within a triangle hence the cowbell rings but no one knows its tone

The eye in the glass, the eye in the Ying and Yang hence the looking glass – eye in the mirror

We see ourselves – the man in the mirror – woman in the mirror but yet we cannot see our evils – the things that we do hence Michael Jackson told us he's talking to the Man in the Mirror and asking him to change his ways but he lost his way he Michael forgot that the devil cannot change. Death cannot change. Death must be true to death. Death must take life in order to keep going and if you are in evils domain the only way you can come out is through death. No one can escape the clutches of death because your life ends when you sign on the dotted line. Yes the death pact because it's death for death and you must drink blood. You must become slaves to evil – Satan as you call him. Even though you want to change you cannot leave – change because that bond – pact is an eternal bond with death. Not even God can break this pact because you have become one of the devils own. There is no resurrection of the dead with this pact because it's absolute and indefinitely final. You signed on the dotted line and made a deal with death.

For all of you that have done this anyone that say they can break this pact is a fool and death is laughing at them. Like I said, not even God can save you because you have become like the living – walking dead. You are the Zombies of death. You have not life therefore life cannot sustain you, you must die with death. You have to die. You are slaves to death and must do the bidding of death. You are workers of death because all your money or all the money that death has offered you you have to hand it back over to death in some way. Hence you are not free. You are bonded – marked – branded with his mark – the mark of the beast – tattoos. No not all have tattoos hence you have henna, bleaching of skin, cosmetic procedures to make your body look like sin – death.

Eve did the same thing and she died much less you. Man she's crying like a bitch because she is the one to receive the souls of her wicked and evil children. There is no life for them hence she gave up life – accepted the offerings of sin and man is she ever paying.

No one can change evil not even God because God do not deal in evil he deals in life. I will forever tell you what belongs to death belongs to death and what belongs to God belongs to God.

God cannot go into deaths land and take out deaths people. No that's not really true because the chosen can and have done it. Moses in Egypt he took life out but good life not bad or evil life hence the color of the Ying and Yang is Light Blue – White and Light Blue and now you know the true color of Life – the life Moses took out of Egypt. And none of you don't even look at me in this land because I haven't seen the good lands of God yet meaning they haven't risen from the depths of the sea as yet. And no the angels of death have not wiped the lands free of its people yet. Soon though, hence the death of all evil life is before 2032.

As humans we forget about evils pay – payment

We forget about our sins and debts hence we rack them up thinking we don't have to pay. We rack them up and say this man died for my sins hence I don't have to pay back my loan with sin. Man oh man are we ever wrong. When we borrow money from the bank do we not have to pay it back so why do you thing when it comes to our sins we do not have to pay?

Oh well I can go bankrupt and I have. True many have but guess what you still have to pay it back. The spiritual world is not like the physical and what you don't pay in the living you must infinitely and indefinitely pay in death – the grave.

No no no. Hear me now no one can die for your sins because we all have sins.

No

No one

But but

Keep believing but I am telling you the infinite truth no one can pay for your sins in the grave. Your sin is your sin. Okay if someone could save you from sin in the grave and per your taught – religious taught – schooling why did someone not save Eve? Why did she have to die? No no no many of you Christians say Jesus was in the beginning with God so if he was why did he not stand up before God and ask God to forgive Eve? Come on now and don't say it is not like that because truth be known you don't know. If I am true love and I am do you not think I would beg God for you. And don't even go there because I have. I have begged God for my homeland. I have begged God for my family – including My Peeps and True Loved Ones. I petition – beg God for them so don't give me any excuse when it comes to asking God for forgiveness when it comes to your people. Like I said true love is rare. It is the greatest gift anyone can have because true love cannot lie. True love cannot hinder nor can it cheat. Let me tell you something evil cannot deal with true love because evil cannot comprehend it – the scope of it. True love is blessed –

divine because it is God's true blessing. If only I could show you. This is how true love is. It cannot deceive and if it did – no I won't even go there because I infinitely and indefinitely know that true love cannot deceive, hurt or lie. True love cannot sin nor is it capable of sin. Well yea because of will. We are capable of Good and Evil. Yes I will get upset and cuss you out wicked when you piss me off but other than that no. I refuse to preach evil because like I said and whether you like it or not you have to know.

Just as how there are certain animals that are unlawful to eat there are certain races that are unlawful to marry. This is the way it was from the beginning of time and this is the way it must be in the end of time – wicked people time.

And you ignorant Black and White people do not go there because like I said the Ying and Yang on another level denotes physical and spiritual death. You cannot change this because none of you know about LIGHT BLUE – not the poison blue ivy.

Like I said we forget that we must repay our debts – sins and the only pay for sin is death.

We pay homage to sin
We glorify death
Partake of death
Drink the blood of death

Now death walks freely. It's polluted the airways and waterways and now we must pay. We must truly die – give death his pay.

Michelle

Dear God today I am in a mellow mood. I feel no emotion for humanity

I have no sympathy for humanity
I will not pray and soil myself – my soul and spirit for them

God today I look forward to the death of death – the death of all evil. I look forward to the death of man – sin

God we know the truth but instead of keeping the truth we abuse it, distort it to justify our wicked and polluted ways – wrongs and for this I feel nothing for humanity nor will I pray to you for them because we all know better.

All the goodness you've given us God we've destroyed it – polluted the land now death truly walks and many more will suffer – die. We gave ourselves over to sin and death now death will take all at will.

Death will destroy us all – well evil not good because Death cannot take the life of good it can only take the life of wicked and evil people.

The Mountain is almost gone God because you are the Mountain and all your goodness will be gone with you because we did not listen – refuse to listen.

Death now comes with the DEATH OF MAN – HUMANITY – ALL EVIL written on his forehead.

I know the hat of death God – true death because I have seen it before.

All we did we did for death now death takes – repays his own at will.

Michelle

These couple of poems is for those boring days when you have nothing to do.

There are no friends to go out with and boredom sets in and trust me I bug God royally. I am a pain to him when I am bored.

Dear God I hope you don't mind because I have included some of my nagging poems to you in this book.

God I have to be me as well as show people just how nagging I can be to you. I do drive you crazy but I know you understand. You have not gotten pissed off at me yet and trust me I don't want you to either.

Hey in all that I do to nag you and defend you my greatest reward is coming to you with everything that is bothering me. Yes I get reprieve but hey you are special to me and yes you will forever be special in my book.

So to my peeps true loved ones and friends enjoy these simple poems of the days when I am bored.

Enjoy

MJ

I Am Bored

God I'm bored
Why am I so bored?
It's Friday
It's cold and I have nothing to do
I'm bored

Even writing bores me
Sex is a bore
Not that I'm having any

Valentine's Day fast approaching
Bet I won't get any flowers
Not even candy
Naa my kids will give me candy
Or a card that they have made

Man life's a bore
When you have no intimate friends
A boyfriend to wine and dine
A boyfriend to look for every now and then

Man I'm boring – not creative
Who in hell sits down and write crap about being bored
Man how bored can one be to be writing trash – crap – rubbish like this.
Am I that boring – wow
Shit for real

Naa its fun
This is my outlet

My sport

But man am I bored
It's Friday and there is nothing to do
Boy am I dull in regards to Valentine's Day
Being an outcast
The ugly ducking
Hell no the swan

Man oh man life sucks when you are alone
Have nothing to do
Frustrating when you are not working
When you are longing to be with someone

I hate these lonely days
Not having someone intellectual to converse with
Hate not having my brain challenged
Hate not having brain busters to challenge
Not that I could
But would
Not to feel smart
But to get my questions answered
But knowing them they would have
A vocabulary all of there own
Memorized all the big words of the dictionary
Boy would they ever make me look stupid
Make them important

But in a nut shell words are words
Some are fancy for those at Yale
Some are simple for me and you

Big words does not denote intelligence
Knowledge on the other hand is key
Communicating words simply for the masses make you smart
The cream of the crop
Corn if you know what I mean
Yeah good food for the heart and soul

But with all that said and with my boredom
I'm bored
Nope television is boring – too much shit on TV
Nah television can expand my mind to much violence. Infinitely too much sex, humongous fakes breasts, booty too. TV has become too fake – deadly
Can't expand my mind
It's the same old same old
Boring and definitely not fun
TV just makes you want to run and infinitely hide

Ah man why couldn't I be in the Caribbean?
Planting yams, tomatoes, cassava, beans – fruit trees
And yes yes yes corn
Love it you know
Would I want to be sipping pina colada?
Indubitably yes
Without the alcohol of course
Took the fun out of it all didn't I
Yeah I'm boring
But yes I would love to be in the Caribbean

Maybe eating some freshly baked chicken wings
Golden and crisp
Yeah you know what I mean

Feet up high listening to the blues
Coltrane, Mahalia, Bo
If not some Prince, Luther maybe not Cold Play – definitely Bob Marley even Tarrus Riley because I am Royal a Nubian Queen
Naa, maybe, depending on the mood
How I feel
How rebellious I want to be
Then ya
Cold Play, Meatloaf – Bat out of Hell - Timeless
Oh Johnny Johnny Johnny – Johnny Gill baby
You can get me in the mood any day, anytime, anywhere
Trey Songz you have nothing on me
This time I'll be the one teaching you a thing or two and trust me I'll have you like Billy Idol
You will be screaming for more in the midnight hour. No lava no hot so – That's Jamaican talk my dear. It sweet and it is infinitely nice. Truss mi you'd be doing a new love song if not dance to the way I'll have you but then ……… no forget you Tyrese will do because ma man can infinitely STAY. Baby you can get down on your knees and beg me any day. You can pray even as long you just STAY….sorry Tyrese you do that to me. You are my love toy – sorry play. So Trey you got to know how to play dis ya

love song and if you can't ride the rhythm then honey you got to go you ain't saying nothing. Not a damned thing. Well you're infinitely gone because a Tyrese you're not. You're not a Tank or even Genuine. Don't take it the wrong way because Genuine is genuine and Tank is a tank because he can hold many things – wata. This is Jamaican lingo you know. TGT baby – Too Good – True yes you can say too good to be true. Wait wait wait
Too many men
I'm not the Weather Girls
Raining men
If it did
I hope it rains me some Shaq, Rock, Bobby Lashley. Let's not forget Shaggy, Denzel baby wooo mama – sorry Mrs. Washington but you have you a fine sexy Nubian King.
Ah Tyrese back to you because you can serenade me anytime – any day. Djimon baby I didn't forget you. You are one sexy African brother and I know why. And on that note I am going to leave well enough alone because if I continue I will infinitely go overboard.

So enough of my infatuation
Whitney Houston – you bring good love
Aretha and Miss Patti aaaaaaah yes Miss Patti LaBelle
Damn girl you be fineeeeeeeeeeeeeeeeeee
Love Ya Mama LaBelle
Yes a vacation is good
Jamaica here I come

Yeah Bobby I will definitely be turning the lights down low in good old JA
Bobby Bobby Yes Mr. Marley get me in the mood.
Three little birds
Yes Bobby take me there
Let your music enchant me, soothe me, bring me true love under the moonlight hour

Do I have to roll a blunt though?
No you sing beautiful music
No blunt needed just you – your soothing voice

Wow I am in the mood
Damn I feel good
But the only problem is I have no one to share it with so forget it Bobby, not turning no damned lights down. This girl is lonely – bored
I'm without a man
Hence my life is
BORING BORING BORING
And yes I am bored – bored bored bored not to death or tears just bored because the day is that damned boring.

Michelle – MJ

What Do I Want To Do

What do I want to do?
What do I want to do?
Kids are home
Yes they are driving me crazy
Couldn't even get rid of my last two

Hey come on
When you are a single mom
You want those occasional weekends to yourself
But then what do I do with my first two

Man oh man even my kids have become boring
Tell me what do I do
I know there is the movies, clubs etc
But movies are limited
Kids don't want to go
They have become as selective as me
Yes boring like me

The don't like to go out
Not even to friends or family's house
Not that there is many
Yes Yes Yes that is good
Good good good it keeps them out of trouble
Yes boring is good Thank God
YA LIKE IT THIS WAY
FORGET BORING

What a Day

What a day
What do I do now?
Can't talk to myself

Games are boring
Can't go for a walk
Too cold outside- that's the trouble the weather

Lord no detest clubs
For me a nice romantic setting will do
Even a steakhouse with a bar
The Keg, Pat and Mario's
God I wonder if they still exist
They use to sell good food
Good liquor too

Man I am behind times
My kids only like Mandarin
That's there thing to go with friends
It's all you can eat you see
And you know kids with a huge appetite
Dem nyam out the salad bar – sorry food bar

But one day for sure I would love to take them to see Newfoundland and Labrador
Oh yeah Nova Scotia
Baby yes Nova Scotia

Man my head is reeling with the thoughts of Nova Scotia
What I would like to do there in beautiful Nova Scotia. So world if I don't get there please go there for me and have just one night of fun and play for me. No people for real. Go buck wild with your mate – partner for me. ***And no – no unfaithful partners.*** Only true partners – mates will do. Don't want no fornication or sin there. You have to stay true to the land – Yea Nova Scotia.
Can't tell you what
Sexual in nature
Yes Yes Yes Nova Scotia
Beautiful Nova Scotia

The screams
The exotic nights of wild and exotic fun with my man well when I get one. Oh man the fun I will have because baby you had better be up to it. Need I remind you of All Night Long – yes Lionel Richie but instead of dancing in the streets we'll be doing it in bed. Oh baby you had better be able to spread me like a sheet and do your thing because trust me 2 – 5 minutes infinitely just won't do.

I would love to see Nunavut

And leave a lasting impression and no not with my behind. Yes too cold but wait no that's another book

The Yukon, North West Territories
If by chance make my way to Alaska just to see the glaciers before they disappear forever

One day Canada one day
I will take you by storm
Even get up enough nerve to go skiing at Blue Mountain, Whistler too
But that's for another time as I map out my adventure in my mind and think about all the naughty things I'd like to do in
Little old Nova Scotia

Michelle - MJ

Prolonged Thought

Yes I am bad but I am bored
Can't get over Nova Scotia
You know what I have got to go there

Newfoundland and Labrador got to go there too
For the fish – cod
Seafood
Can you believe many of us Canadians have not discovered the beauty of Canada – landscape that is
Over thirty years I have been here
Never explored the country
Have to because Canada has some truly beautiful
scenic paradise – places – multicultural haven.
And yes people despite the way I feel about the land – the coldness of the land there are some beautiful places to see.

I might not infinitely love the land and will never infinitely endorse it but I cannot be ungrateful. The land has been good and bad to me well more bad than good but I have to play my part no matter how small. So don't judge me if I don't infinitely endorse it and from reading above you know why.

Yes a lot of the people are friendly
And no we don't live in Igloo's
I never realized the diversity of the land
The different cultures living as one
Yes we have issues
Racism still exist but that is everywhere in every homeland
Take a look in your own country
Your own family
Not everybody is going to like each other – be on one accord

If you need direction to get from point A to B

We are only too happy to give it to you
If you smile and say good morning
You will get that friendly smile and a hearty good morning back

You can go anywhere in the country and feel at home
You will be served
Canadians are all out friendly
Way too friendly and that's a good thing

Yes our winters are cold
Yes the winters are too long for me
But there is much to do like
Skiing at Blue Mountain
Let's not forget skiing in British Columbia
There is snow boarding, ice fishing, ski doing
Oh lord let's not forget hockey
Oh man do Canadian's ever love hockey
There is basket ball but hockey takes precedence
Sorry Shaq because in my book you are all that
Man oh man what I wouldn't do to have a date with you
sorry Mrs. O'Neil just a childhood fantasy
But can I borrow him for a night or two
Sorry just kidding
You are his wife and I have to have respect
Because respect is due

Now I have lost track
Sorry Canada
Come on world take a chance
Visit Canada especially Nova Scotia before Canada – the true North is gone
Your life will change because the North will be no more.

Michelle

My Collective – The Dark Side of Me – Part One

Oh God I am bored
Are you here yet?

God I am bored
Entertain me
Be all that I need you to be on this day

Godddddd I am bored
Are you on your way yet?
Are you close to my home?

Gooooodddddddd I am bored
So since I am bored I am going to truly nag you

The house is boring and I so don't want to clean. I want to go shopping in Jamaica because I need a couple of hours in the sun

Goddddddddd I am bored
Are you here yet?
Where are you?
I need you
Gooooodddddddddd I am bored
Are you here yet?
Are you close by?
How far are you?
Can't take this boredom no more
Goooddddddd I feel like I am going to go insane because I am oh so bored.

No I don't want to write a love story all I want to do is go shopping with you and my family somewhere

Godddddd I am bored
My house is boring and no I don't want to play video games it's too boring. Don't want to watch television either it too is boring hence I hardly watch it – can't stand it so I am bugging you.

Need to have a channel just for me. A channel that only plays the oldies Spiderman the vintage cartoons Scooby Doo, He-man. Fat Albert, Sanford and Son, Good Times, Wonder Woman, Isis, Buck Rogers, X-men. Can't stand some of the crap they have on TV now a days. Give me CSI Miami, Criminal Minds any day. Bionic Woman, Bionic Man, Charles Angels yes even Eddie Murphy too but not the crap he has now couldn't stand Norbert glad it flopped. Definitely give me more Madea yes Tyler Perry is the bomb he can play my Madea any day yes in real life yes in the drag because he's that funny. Tyler don't get a sex change though and become a thing because sex changes are just nasty and more than sinful in my book and God's book. Trust me you are truly hilarious and if you

have a sex change you will know when your world falls apart just how sinful you have become.
Goddddddd I am bored
Are you here yet?
Where are you and don't tell me you are stuck in traffic?
Goddddd I am bored
Where are you I am getting impatient?

Godddd I'm bored
Where are you God?
I am bored and you are not here yet

MICHELLE

God you know I am going to nag you because I am bored and I have nothing to do

God I am bored
I need you right here
Right now in my life

I thought we were pals
You would always be there for me so where are you cause I am deafly bored I need something to do

I want to go shopping
Godddddd I don't want to talk to no one. I just want to nag you and yes I am bored

Goodddddd why aren't you calling me?
Why are you shutting me out? You know how nagging and pestering I can be when I am bored

Godddddd I want to go shopping can you please come and give me some money. Better yet since I am bored you have to onbore me. You have to make me happy. A trip a good and blessed trip to Jamaica will do. You have to prepare everything though and you cannot let it be 6 months from now I want this trip right now so you had better prepare your concord yes the luxury one and come whisk me away

Goddddd I am bored and yes I am becoming demanding because you know me when I am bored.

I need to be pampered
Yes taken care of

I need to be treated more than a queen because yes I am bored too bored and you are the only one I can nag and demand.

Not that you will listen to my demands and nagging but I am going to nag you anyway because I have nothing better to do.

Goddddd I am bored
Too bored
Why can't you satisfy my desires? Come on don't let me be mad at you. I am tired of being bored and look you are doing nothing about it.

Godddddddddddddd I'm bored and I am so not going to stop nagging you until you give me what I want or you get pissed off at me.
Godddddddddddddddddddddddd
Goddddddddddddddddddddddddd I'm bored. Where are you? I need to go shopping and yes I need you to take me to dinner.

MICHELLE

God am I getting to you yet?
Well I am bored and I need you to make me happy

Why are you so stubborn?
Why do you have to make me bored and yes even boring?

Goddddd I am so bored that I have become so nagging

God why are you ignoring me in my time of boredom and loneliness?

God I am bored
No I do not want to call anyone to gossip
Talking on the phone is boring and no I do not have a cell phone don't want one yet for now my home phone will do

Too much bills I don't go anywhere persay so why do I need a cell phone so like I said my home phone will do.

Nope detest face book
Don't understand twitter
Emails are only for business and yes I know I am that boring
Hate watching TV more times. Yes I have MSN to get my local and international news fix – information and yes even that becomes boring at times.

No I don't really watch the news anymore my favorite anchors are gone so why should I watch TV? Some of the newscaster's are boring don't even know a thing.

Yes they can't grip me. Shoot I don't even want to see them they have no journalistic savvy. Give me the original anchors maybe then I will sit and watch TV the news that is and yes more often.

Yes TV has become crappy. Too much sex violence and crap. Now they have children wanting and playing the roles of adults before their time. Crap crap crap. What happened to shows like the Wonder Years, Cosby, A different World, good family shows that depict family in a positive light. Bring back Leave it to Beaver, hey what happened to Hopei, shows like I Love Lucy Green Acres?

Godddd I am bored. Bored of the new shit why can't you bring back the old yes shows that depict true family values and issue instead of leaving us with the crap they are showing – bombarding us with?

MICHELLE

Yes God I took a deep breath because I am bored. You know what Valentine's Day is coming soon and guess what I am going to be bored too

In truth I wasn't thinking about it
Hopefully Valentine's Day 2013 will bring me good cheer.

Yes on this particular Valentine's Day I want a beautiful all diamond ring. No it's not a need it's a want so God you had better start creating and making because this ring I want from you. And no you can't say I did not give you a year because I gave you over a year's notice because today is February 04, 2012

I won't even tell you what I want and need for my birthday it's too soon but it had better be special

Yes I am bored and I am giving you ample time. And you better not give me a ring of yellow gold and diamond because you know how I detest yellow gold. You know yellow gold is worthless in your kingdom it is discarded

Pure silver or white gold will do but never yellow plain out nasty

Yes yes yes I know I am picky but so are you. You're more picker than me

Yes you're too picky so let's not talk about me I guess we are both picky people

Yes I am feeling a bit better but I still would have preferred it if you fired up – started up your luxury concord and truly take me to dinner in Paris no not Jamaica because the next trip to Jamaica I want to go with a special someone yes human and I know you can't be human to please me. The planet is laden with filth and I cannot let you dirty yourself.

Besides I know the distance between us
The space and time
Yes the garbage in between us

The land you reside in is clean and mine is laden with filth. You know what God this is why you need to prepare the perfect place for me and you. One that is void of filth. A place where no evil can come in; a place built for me and you and don't even tell me this cannot be done. Need I remind you of the island rising in the land of Kenya?

Baby no more distance between us.
True love always and yes just to let you know I AM STILL BORED.

MICHELLE

God since I am bored and you are not coming to dinner- you are not taking me to dinner you owe me big time and trust me I will be collecting hence I will hold you accountable for ignoring me.

God do you know how bored I am? I am not lonely just bored.

I am going to wash my dishes because dishes are in my sink but you still owe me big time for not truly taking me to dinner

No smiley on your part you owe me big time and yes I can hold you accountable for sin. Yes leaving me bored and not truly being there for me when I nag you

No you don't take the ear plugs out of your ears you know how devastating my boredom can be

I told you everyone knows that I rely on you for everything. You cannot say you didn't know because you know you are my ALL and I do everything in you
Matter of fact to so far everything has been about my boredom what about you.
Oh man have mercy Boo what about your boredom?

Your happiness

Oh God I wasn't thinking about you

Yes I know Ya think

Well I am sorry for neglecting you and trust me I will be making it up to you

Need to get us a fruit basket or a fruit tray at the grocery store. Hopefully I can do this on Valentine's Day. I am also hoping that you will lay with me and we can enjoy ourselves while watching a good movie on tv.

Boo I am truly sorry for neglecting you and only thinking of myself my boredom because deep down you are bored too.

MICHELLE

God I am going to nag you because I have nothing better to do

It's Friday and it's cold outside

Gooooddddd I am so going to nag you. Yes I am going to bug you because I need something

You know what I need but today and I am going to nag you. I need a vacation

I want to go home but in truth that's not what I am nagging you about

Gooooodddddddd ah forget it I am so not going to nag you. You're a good friend and no I am not lonely just wanted to nag you but changed my mind.

Lovey it's Friday the weekend is near and I just want to make it clear it's going to be boring for me unless you do something. You have something planned for me.

God don't want to call anyone. Talked too much today with family and friends from home so no just want to be me just you and me two loving friends just having fun.

MICHELLE

God you know you are going to have to make me see you more often

You know if I keep this talk up people might think I am crazy

They might think I need a loony bin because they cannot comprehend my type of writing or the relationship I have with you

It's weird
Some might say I need a psychotic help, hey others might want to psychoanalyze me. Cool but who would be playing the fool? Certainly not me

Have mercy God so forgive me because trust me I would have a field day

Textbook bullshit verses God smarts. Classic – a classic confrontation between God and man.

MICHELLE

God I can't nag you anymore because I am no longer bored

Thank you for the groceries I needed it.
Man you surprised me. Truly thank you because I was not expecting it.

You did take me shopping by letting my son's girlfriend and son go shopping for me

I have groceries now truly truly infinitely truly thank you. You saw my needs and delivered

Wow you are amazing God

Here I was nagging you I even told you I would hold you accountable and I can't. I got groceries. You provided for me and my family.

Infinitely truly thank you. I know I cannot repay you for what you did but what I do hope is that my thank yous are good enough on this day February 04, 2012.

MICHELLE

Lovey thank you for the goodness and blessings you have showered me with

Truly thank you for being there for me – having my back

On this day I truly with you were near for me to hug and kiss you and say thank you face to face.

God you are my Lovey and you are truly loved

You are truly cherished

You are truly there for me

You are my lifeline
My All
My Everything
You are the one I run to – come to with every thing

Thank you truly thank you for providing for my needs. Truly thank you for being my All – My Everything.

MICHELLE

As time moves forward and the scope of the earth fades one has to think about tomorrow and the generations left behind. The generations of our children and grandchildren and what they will inherit. What turmoil they have to face as they clean up the mess of my generation. What will they become? Will they cry for death or even run to the mountain as the bible say to find a hiding place from what is to come. The hell on earth they will have to face. Hell on earth due to the greed of man.

The World Cry Out

The world cries out
Water will not be the downfall of humans on earth
Water will not be the downfall of our planet earth
Humanities sin and greed – vanity will be

World food supply in decline
Poisoned waterways – blood water - diamond
Global starvation will become the new cry – revelation. Cannibalism the eating of human flesh will become the new norm – food – sustenance
Hatred sustained
Babies dying everywhere
Single motherhood have now become the norm
Babies raising babies
The extension of the teenage years

Lawless societies everywhere
Man have out numbered the trees of the planet we call earth
No space to plant
No place to live
Empty factories

Ah yes the human factories – scavengers looking for a clean home – food to eat

The fallen dollar bill
Heat burn the land
Grass and trees no longer grow
No medicine to produce to heal and cure the sick
Economic ruin everywhere

Money no longer valued
Can't buy anything
Companies shut down – nothing to produce or reuse

The poor man cry
The rich man die
The loss of life
Everything

Drinking water becoming scarce
Pollution escalating
No logical solutions
Empty political system
Failing and falling judicial system
War waged on drug lords
The new drug that kill at will
New hallucinogens – Zombieism
Cannibalism man jumping over walls

All who kill to produce, produce to kill will see their deaths before them and there won't be a damned thing they can do about it because all must go through the gates of hell.

There is no turning back for the wicked
No going forward for the wicked

Greed lives everywhere in them hence they produce to kill – take the lives of man

Technological advances
Biological warfare
Human trafficking
Genocide

Where do we go from here?
Children talking
Walking
Confused

Parents aren't listening
World in disarray
Need a new world order?
One of truth – true peace

Bullies and vanity on the rise
It's the new in thing – norm
Facial reconstruction
The price paid for perfection beauty – sin
Yes the price of ugliness because all want to look like sin – the sinful one – Satan

Here today gone tomorrow because soon there will be none

Who will take a stance?
Who will record it?
Turn back the clock
Start at the beginning
Cleanse the deep
Renew Mother Earth

Theories fly

Aliens – well that's another chapter
Global Warming
Ozone depleting
Great Barrier Reefs fleeing
Ice age – Glaciers receding

Water – polluting – oils spills everywhere
Death waiting
Laughing
Anti-Christ walking

Faith sealed at the hands of man
At the hands of our own selfish needs
Our own greed

Who will cry for man?
Who will plea for them?
Who will reform them – carry on the truth?
Ah yes the faith of man
They said they have books
Scrolls
Scrolls of God but in truth they have scrolls of men
Men that deceive – lie – bargain away their lives to the dead – death to save their own. But I guess they never knew that no one can trust death because death is not life it is death and it can only take life not give it. Yes it's crying time, man will weep and mourn because they did trust the deceitful one – the great Liar of Old that which you call Satan.

Michelle

The Faster We Grow

The faster we grow
The more destructive we become
The more intolerance grow
Hate spread

Fast foods
Fast cars
Fast money
Fast love
Fast sex
Fast drugs
Fast everything and the more inhuman we become

Diseases grow
Pesticides
New life
New germ
Body cannot control
Cannot kill
Ward off

The looking glass is broken
No one wants to see who
Or what we have become

Outdated like a computer

TV
The stereo
CD's

Take a look and see me
The generation gap
Space exploration
The extinction of man – humanity
The wonders of the mind
We are being controlled
Manipulated by TV
New gadgets
New things

Illusion spreads
Confusion ill perceived
We have become the walking dead
All including the All have become understated – an understatement
A game – a farce

All is written
The game is over
Man terminated
Machines lives on
A new generation is born

Michelle

Technology

Technology increasing
Man depleting
Technology moves on

New phones
New games
TV's
New house
New males
New females
NEW EVERYTHING

New technology to start cars
Turn your lights on and off
Technology to drive you here there and everywhere
Got to wonder if there is a new you
A new me
A switch to turn me on or off
No not the sex toy

The race is on
Genetic payload – overload
Mapping the human gnome
Human guinea pigs
Racial divide
Racial destruction

Chemical payload
Organic freefall
Nuclear disaster

Tragedy
Natural species irradiated
Trees
Plants
Animals
Humans alike all gone

The power struggle still rages on
Who will be the first in the new kingdom?
Pity all is lost
Times up
Game over
Humanity truly gone

Michelle

Concepts of Female/ Male - Humanity

FEMALE

MALE

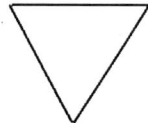

Both triangles
Both 180 degrees

One negative
One positive
Law of attraction

Neutral the same
Female   Female
Male   Male
Something Missing
Genetic or chemical
The same--------one---------like matter
Like relationship

Mind – curious – want
Outside scope   BI-does not fall
Into the same bracket as above
State of mind
Want – to try
Fit in
Go with the crowd

Michelle

Concept of Perfection

Circle

Perfect to man
Has no beginning
Has no end
Or
No starting point
No ending
Can be cut to make a straight line
Therefore imperfect

A dot is more perfect than a circle
True to life
Cannot be cut – broken
Cannot be erased
If erased impression still there

Square

A square is perfect in the eyes of sin because it represents the double cross
Four equal sides
Can contain a triangle and a circle but can it truly
Can be broken
Imperfect containment unit
Therefore God cannot be a circle or square.
God – Life cannot be contained but death – sin can

The square is man's body

Because it is a containment unit for the soul or spirit – evil spirits – wicked and evil people
The square is a trap because it represents the stage when evil came into being – the birth of evil and his people hence it is the cross – crosses the representation of evil societies – churches that pay homage to their demons – gods.

The circle is the soul or spirit
The square does not die but in retrospect it can die does die in flesh but not in spirit

The square is not perfect it is 24 – a day in time – the time and day of the enemy – light and day – evil spirits – a time to die

The bones are still there after the body decays it is the true prison for the spirit. The cage that holds our spirit captive within our polluted – decaying bodies

The circle revolves – the spirit or soul
It vibrates
Must find its original energy source
Life – The True and Living God
Therefore the soul can contain both the triangle and circle at the same time within the same day so therefore a square is not perfect it is imperfect the source of all evil.

Perfection continued

A man or woman *cannot be 360 degrees by themselves*
Combined they become one - 360 degrees in strength and power meaning unified in love - truth

Male +	Fe	=	Female
He +	S	=	She
He +	R	=	Her
Man +	Wo	=	Woman

Males	Negative
Females	Positive

Females	Negative
Males	Positive

But in truth males cannot be positive they have to be the negative one. They go down not up hence the inverted triangle.

1 (one)	Dominant
1 (one)	Passive

1 (one)	Giver
1 (one)	Receiver
Stronger	Female

Males give to female
Female are the receiver
Hence when both are joined they become 360 Degrees in sex – foreplay – the love game. They become one but can never be one. Will always be two but like union the same depending on how you

look at the universe and its make up in regards to good and evil – the Ying and Yang.

Males can never become 360
Therefore power struggle
Man will always seek power
Domination
Good verses Evil syndrome

As to creation Genesis is false-inaccurate
The God in Genesis is a fake
He can create
But cannot procreate by himself
In Genesis it said **"Let us make man in our image**
In the image of God created he them
Male and female created he him
Therefore there had to be a female present
The fusion of semen with the female zygote
Therefore creating
Birthing male and female children
So therefore Genesis does not substantiate the One God theory at all
There was exchange of seminal fluid
The wild thing happened
Love
Perfect
Wow factor – Sex
Intercourse
Yes this is absolute truth
Absolute knowledge
Perfection at it's very best.
This is life – true life

Michelle

Life

Heat – absolutely necessary
Body cannot function without heat

Need heat to survive
Need heat to procreate
Need heat to produce

Friction produces heat
Heat is one of the key ingredients to life
Sustaining, maintaining and creating life

Therefore Males are the reactors – penis
Females are the conductors – vagina

Male penis – friction
Push pull effect
Produces heat

Force – speed is another element
The more speed the more friction
More friction
More heat
Greater pleasure
A higher high
Therefore heat, speed-force-friction
Key component in reproduction
Woman is the conductor
The receiver of force
The ultimate giver of life
Birth

Therefore there must be a giver and receiver in life
Ultimately the receiver becomes the giver
And the giver becomes the receiver.

Michelle

Tired

I am tired of the nonsense
Tired of the religious divide
Tired of religious fraud

Tired of a God that's a fraud
Tired of worshipping Pagan Gods
Gods I cannot see
Gods that cannot love
Gods that relish in our struggles
Gods who cannot hear

Humanity struggling
Wars divide
We spread hate
Propaganda
Yeah you know religion

Tired of the fights
The feuds
Tired of my religion is right
Your religion is wrong
Tired of the you're going to hell if you don't come my way

What makes your religion right?
Burn the damned bible and walk the right way
Turn back from false teachings and get the right book

Celebrate God – The True and Living God the right way

Turn back from the wrong path
Celebrate God your way because no religion is right when it comes to the true and living God and you all know this – hence revelations told you about the churches
Walk in your truth
Honesty and Integrity
Walk with faith
You will find the right way

Come celebrate with God in his original form
The true way
The way God ordained it to be

Michelle

The darkness come there's no place to hide – run
No laughter is there just hopelessness
A society overrun by violence, hate, crime, murder
Earth has become the killing field for men
So the darkness come and brings about more doom and gloom

Michelle

My pain is not your pain
Mama cries
Weeps and mourn
Ball till daylight come

Her child is gone
Gone senseless violence – the gun

She weeps and mourn
Mama cry
Her child is gone
Slain by violent and vicious men
Demons – the devils own
His children

Mama cry, mama cry
Mama weep and mourn for the life of her child
The one lost at the hand of the gun – shot dead by men without mercy.
Shot dead by ugly and sinful demons
The devils spawn hence mama cry, cry for the life of her only son – daughter.

Michelle

My Truths

Give a man or woman knowledge he will use it for his or her own gain.

Give a man or woman knowledge they will use it to destroy.

Give a man or woman God they will use him to deceive.

Give a man or woman hope they will cry.

Take the truth from him or her and they will become lost.

Take away the spirit or soul and death comes.

But yet with all these gifts
Gifts of knowledge

Man cannot conceive the concept of nothing – darkness

Cannot conceive or see that all theses things was given to us by the True and Living God

Cannot conceive that knowledge is a gift from God and if we do not use it wisely we will truly become forever lost.

We need to now use or knowledge wisely lest we become like those left behind by Noah
Lost
Gone forever!
Forgotten
Knowledge is one of the keys to life
It is a gateway to God

With knowledge all is revealed and opened onto you

With knowledge you cannot be lost

Will never be lost because you now know

There are no beliefs in knowledge because knowledge is set it cannot be rocked

To know is to live hence knowledge

To believe is to die hence we die

It is a foolish man that says death is pretty when he sees the ugliness of sin all around – each and every day

It is a foolish man who thinks he can buy beauty just look at the skin – the fading and ugliness of him

True beauty is within hence a man without a good soul cannot see or comprehend true beauty – the beauty within

It is said a man that does foolish things is a fool. I guess he did not stop to think and see the foolishness of this world.

A wise man look and see but it is a foolish man that plows ahead without knowing.

It is a foolish man or woman that raise his child in sin and believes they can become good

It is a foolish woman that goes to bed with thorns and expect roses in the morn – morning

A good man knoweth the gift of God hence he cherish all that God has given him including his wife

Michelle

It's Funny

It's funny how the world is changing
Funny how far man has come to know nothing
How pig headed we are
How blinded we've become

Teaching has become a chore
We have learnt nothing from the past
The extinction of life
Chaos

Earth
Fire
Air
Water
The four elements
All distinct
All equally important
Human
All can be found in man
The composite of the earth
The union of man and woman
Life and death – union

The wow factor for some
Our saving grace

There is nothing wow about it

Basic knowledge
Crazy thought for some
The evolution of man
The maintenance of man

From angels to humans
From humans to dust
From dust to life
Death for some
Life moves forward in a different form
The next stage in life
Without form or void – spiritual life

Where does that energy go?
Who knows?
Nothing matters anymore
We move on
Wage war
Spread hate
Destroy
Just another chapter in human form
Human life
Form of life

Michelle

Like Solomon

Like Solomon all I see around me is vanity
Vanity of spirit
Vanity of soul
Self hate

No matter how much you have
How little you have
The mind cannot be satisfied
It will always seek more
Want more
Need more

Greed all around me
It controls mother earth
Destroys it

All I see is man wanting what the other has
There is much jealousy
Vexation of spirit as Solomon puts it

We kill to have what the other man has
Steal, rob and rape to gain ground
Only to get nothing in return

We deceive our fellow man
Live our lives in greed - lies
Only to lose our souls in the end - die

The one thing I know
We have it all and will eventually lose it all
Die and another man or woman enjoys what you have left behind. Yes enjoy it all

All that we lust after is nothing but vanity
Hatred of the spirit
Confusion of the heart
Greed at its highest form – grandiose scale

Everything including the God we worship is vanity of spirit – vexation of the heart
An abomination of spirit because hatred still lingers in the heart – mind and spirit

Fears are spread
Races believing they are better than the other
Racial divide
The conquering and domination of man – humanity

We've become slaves
We're bought and sold
The mind unfolds
Dictates your actions
Command you at will
Controls

The concept of God is vexation of spirit
We seek but yet we cannot find
Fantasies and myths take precedence
Preached
Gone like the wind
Wild

We pray to false gods
Worship idols and call them gods

But yet with all that we do we cannot see the destruction of self – our owns deaths

So we continue to pray in vain
Hoping waiting for a god that is truly not there so we rebel – sin even more

We talk, we fight – spread hate even more
We become even more vile – sinful
We become lover of self – self praise
We become vainer – the lust and thirst for perfection – ultimate beauty

Yes we alter self and think this is good but in the end we find out that we were wrong hence we cry – die a harsher death because we committed one of the carnal sins – vanity

We have laws but for the elect they are not governed by these laws because they can kill at will – send troops in another man's land to wipe them clean off the face of this earth
Yet they preach and teach thou shalt not kill
They justify themselves – their wrongs with books of sin – lies

They cannot see that THOU SHALT NOT KILL goes for all – all of humanity and nothing that man do can justify sin because we live in sin hence we die

We teach sin hence we die
We take life – kill hence we die

All that we do we do in sin hence we all have to die – pay for our sins

One law does not apply to whomever we feel like – it applies to all

You cannot kill and expect to get right because death cannot be justified nor does death seek justification for himself or what he does. He death must live by the law and laws and that is to take live whenever we sin hence we die

No human being can justify death because it is said the wages of sin is death

So when you sin you have get paid and no lawyer, no spirit, no one can save you for this sin because IT IS LAW. We know the law and it said THE WAGES OF SIN IS DEATH so all who sin must die and no one can change this or petition death or God for this. The law is the law and what is written cannot be change by spirit or men because it is the law like I said and it is written hence it is law.

Death talks and death shows you
You accepted death – the offerings of death and death kills you – must kill you

We've all forgotten that there is no life in death just death and it is lifeless hence we die in flesh and die a severe and painful death in the spirit.

Michelle

Lies

Aah what lies have been told
Manipulation
Confusion

The challenge is nice
Man walk in fear
We write
Lure
Talk but no one listens
Cares

Famine is near
Water supply short
Climate change
Global war

Economic crisis
Economic collapse
Tribal war

No one is safe
The door is ajar
Who will go?
Who will stay under the stars?

Worlds colliding
Dirty words of hate muttered
Sun burnt out

No more crescent moon
Darkness renewed
No food to eat
Water to drink
Hell unleashed upon earth
No farmers to till the land
No harvest to reap
No corn to sow

Generations gone
False prophet's retreat
No more lies to spread
Salvation gone
Doom and gloom

Death knocks no more
Does not walk
Does not talk
Show his face no more

Life as we know it eradicated
Gone

All that's left are outdated computers
Machines
Bones from a civilization that once was
But now gone

Will a new generation be born?
Will they follow in our footsteps?

Will they heed the warnings?
Follow the truth
Will they learn to do right and not wrong?
Do that which is the truth
Who knows?
Who's to tell?
Humanity is gone
Extinct because they would not listen

Death came for a time
They followed him
He took what he wanted – needed
He did his job

Now man is extinct and all that is left are dry bones of sinful nations
Rebellious kids
Racist bastards
Death's own

Michelle

Don't

Don't pick my brain cause it's empty
Don't give me the bible because it is filled with lies, sin and deceit

Recreated to use my family's history against me
Recreated for me to follow you and your gods – sin
Recreated to deceive me
Recreated for me to worship you
Recreated for me to lose my soul
Recreated for me to die a painful death
Recreated for me to disrespect the True and Living God
Recreated for me to bring God shame and disgrace

Don't tell me Adam and Eve was the first creation
I know otherwise
They are the children of sin
The mother and father of all that is evil – humanity
They are the mother and father of all things inhuman – wicked
They are the mother and father of sin – death
I know the creative fraud
The living – lying game to keep us fed

Adam and Eve could never be the first because there were other people before them
Other Kings and Queens
Princes and Princesses

Yes they polluted the earth
Causing everything to fall into chaos
Causing man to burn – sin and die

Lies lies lies and more lies

Seek the truth it is encoded within
You do not know of our elegant and righteous history and could never live it because it is not about you but about me – my ancestral history
The true kings and queens before me hence sin can never tell me about good because there is no good in sin - evil

Genesis is not the beginning could never be because God's original creations hath and had no DNA hence you cannot trace them or see them
Creation existed long before you
Before the birds

Before the colliding of atoms
The containment of energy
Forming of man

Time has moved forward
Accelerated
Earth has shifted
Man has devolved
Evolved
Revolved
Not moving forward but staying the same

All that is was
All that was is

Genetic manipulation
Nothing new
Was from the days of old
Egypt specifically

With heat comes life
Maintained in part by the sun and moon

Heat and fire are one of the keys because all life form need it – cannot comprehend it hence we destroy what we do not know

Man cannot comprehend God or the scope of God because man cannot see beyond the flesh – his prison – his cell – physical make up

All that was taught was taught to imprison us hence the spirit is imprisoned by the flesh

We've closed off the gateway to God hence we live in sin and cannot return

Yes for you who want to know the gateway to God is your soft spot – like that in a baby's head

Because our soft spot is closed off we no longer have that true connection to God – we are stuck in our prison – the prison of flesh – deceit

Yes this is why the spirit cannot leave at will hence we die and feel greater pain because of unclean spirits – sinful acts we have committed here on earth

Energy greater than the sun and moon
Without the All we die
We hath not life
Energy – the spirit goes back to his or her beginning
The source whether good or evil

Michelle

Numbers

Numbers numbers numbers
Mathematics mathematics mathematics
Aah how ignorant we have become

Many love it
Many hate it
Many kids say there is no meaning behind it
We are not going to use it in our daily lives

Insolent
Ignorant
Arrogance on their part

Everything in life is based on numbers
Shapes
Perfection

Life itself is based on numbers
Time is based on numbers
The seasons
Harvesting
Growing
All based on numbers

Everything in the universe is based on numbers
Even God himself is based on numbers – Time

Numbers numbers numbers
Must take shape
Shapes must take the form of numbers

Numbers numbers numbers
Life and death
All based on numbers
Numbers numbers numbers

Michelle

My Love

My love why have you gone from me
Why have you put your tails between your legs and flee
Why have you run from here?
Left me alone
Left me to crash and burn

I finally know the truth
Your love was never ever true

Yes you ran
But I am still here
I refuse to crash and burn

I know the lies
Lies I've had to learn
But now I know better
I know your meanness
I know you truly cannot give
Truly cannot care

Yes you're gone and my life is slowly getting better
One day I will be back on my feet
Because you can't always keep a good brother or sister down

Michelle

Peace and Love

Peace love and harmony – truth
Everything was so peaceful before you came along
Many stories have been told
Over the centuries they have changed
You have become deified
Worshipped in temples, churches and synagogues, mosques – the works

Many have made you there god
Professing they are worshiping the Holy One
The Most High
God
Jehovah
YahYah
Yallahs
Allah
Allelujah

Things have definitely changed
I give you props for keeping the truth at bay
You are good
Better than the mind
Because without you the truth would be known

I can't blame you though
You have your job to do and you are correct
Man only love the Supreme Being for what he can give to them

Isaiah was also correct because this book is about you written by you for you hence the book of Isaiah is a lie, a fake like you. Hence true evil is she in the physical and he in the spiritual hence man beat woman into submission in the physical. You want all the power and glory hence woman cannot change she determines life – the giver of life. You need her she does not need you hence woman cannot change XX but you can because you are a part of woman hence you are XY – you change. There are 3x's to one of you hence the female gene outnumber you 3 to 1. Yes it's the triangle but on a different level it's the trinity – the 3 daughters of sin your 666 hence you call it the mark of the beast – the trinity – your father son and holy ghost. But you cannot forget the one hence 1 the number one represent you. You are the 3 in one to some but you cannot be 3 in 1 because 3 can never define you because you can only have 3xy and no anomaly.

You cannot lie
You can only tell the truth
The truth of your knowledge
What you know
The truth of your environment
Your enslavement

Therefore you are no different from us
According to the book – the bible you can take life
So you are like unto the angel of death
Each and everyday people kill for you
Die

Confusion must stop
You were given an allotted time
You have proven your point
Man cannot worship God the way they are suppose to because the true and living God requires no worship – only praise – true thank yous
You've also forgotten that God never said in the beginning worship ME so keep on stealing because you are the true identity thief. But know you are Satan – evil and you cannot steal God's identity no matter how hard you try.

God is God he does not deal in stink – death

God is pure he cannot age because God is truth and true cannot grow old nor can truth die

Death ages hence we go old and die
Death lies hence we tell lies and believe in lies

Yes Satan you've become old, wrinkly – decayed – dilapidated – hence you stink and when evil passes through your home or even enter your home they literally smell like filth – shit and some smell like decaying – rotting sulfur.

God – The True and Living God will forever stay true and good. He will forever be young because like I've said God – The True and Living God cannot age. No wrinkles have he hence he is Life – Good and True.

So as life moves forward all that you do in sin is ride on the coat tail of the True and Living God and trust me very soon you will be tossed off and the world will see you for who you truly are. Many will cry but that is the price they paid for vanity – external beauty.

Michelle

Concept of the beginning

This planet is just a travelling ground
A vacation away from home
A planet of many races
Faces
Fascinating places

Many kingdoms have come and gone
Many perish
Many flourish
Many left to decay
Rot
Burn

The richness of the land is there
The minerals left here to enjoy
Maintain and sustain
This was once a beautiful paradise
A tropical oasis until man came
We are the planet under the moon
A planet with many moons – stars
Yes the planet to come to for a true honeymoon

Many stayed
Changed there shape because the climate was good
Good for the many hues – genes

As time moved on we became trapped
Trapped forever
Due to volcanic eruptions
Meteor showers
Showers that moved the earth out of orbit
Out of its original space

We could no longer get home

We became giants
Humanoids
Human – a different type of being

We became the children of the lost
We had to make earth our new home

We existed in peace for many thousands years
Trillions if you would like to know
We lived under water
Building cities, carving the blueprint for the planet you now know as earth. We could not die but when the rift came we began to die due to pollution – humans polluting baby earth

Over the millions of years many died
We no longer became important
Things were changing at a rapid rate
Things we did not foresee
Our eventual extinction – rebirth

We lost our way of thinking
Communicating
Traditions we tried to keep but as the earth moved closer to the sun many moved further from the clan
Many moved to the surface
We could no longer live underwater
Could no longer live in the sea
Breathe as fishes do
Lived on mountains like goats away from the wickedness that was now plaguing the earth – hence they called us Capricorns – beings that went from mountains to seas and rivers – water

We developed cites

Even build a garden of peace to carry on traditions that remained
It was a garden we could call home
A garden we hoped would one day take us home

But all was lost when we once again was hurled closer to the sun
Even further away from our universe
Our perfect way of life – home

We have seen many races come
Races that lived outside our enclosed garden
Races that was not like us
Races that loved violence
Evil
Races that were master deceivers
Races that loved to hate
Wage war

They were different
They were the whisperers – like unto snakes – vipers. A race so beautiful to look at many wanted to join them.
Many did
Many had children with them

The children changed
They lost their identity
Lost their way home
Their ability to communicate with each other
Their ability to communicate with the holy one – God

They lost their ability to tell time
They lost their ability to keep the balance of time on earth

They lost their ability to protect themselves – man
They lost their ability to protect the earth
They lost their ability to protect humanity for earth's gravitational pull – negative forces that pull the earth to align with more negative forces – evil.

Those that were pure we kept in the garden
We were few in numbers
But was outnumbered by those who left the fold

We were in heaven but that was not to last
Things became hard outside the garden
Dryness was upon the land
Because of our kind hearts we let one back in
Our garden became quickly polluted
Everything suddenly changed
Evil was within
We got kicked out due to compassion of the heart
One with a lustful heart
One that only saw the beauty of the skin
Not the beauty of the heart
Due to one act we became impure
Our body and mind became polluted
Yes she was one of us
Our own kind
We thought she wanted all that was good
But we were wrong because she was the true deceitful one. She wanted to be like love – the true Holy One. She did not know all good life is from God and can never be evil. She must be good hence all the children of God are good and not evil. They are females of a different kind hence evil tries to mimic them – take their identity – then kill them.
We the band of god – good had to leave because the land could not house us due to its sinful and filthy nature. The sinful and dirty nature of man because

they caused the earth to become dirty – riddled with their filth – sins.

We were now the outcast
It only took one to cause a chain reaction
One that desire the flesh of another
One that was deceived by the cunning one
The Mind/Soul
That was apart of the trick
Apart of the game
Many became slaves and are slaves until this day

In that purified garden we found we could never die
We did everything we had to
To keep ourselves pure
But that was not to be
The circle became broken because we let him in
We listened to the whispers of the heart
Let the whispers subdue us
Con us
Steal our identity
Rape and pollute us

He talked a new form of sexual pleasure
A pleasure that caused families
Pleasures that caused division within the home
Pleasures that caused men and woman to find gratification elsewhere
Women no longer wanted there husbands
Men no longer wanted there wives
Causing us to pollute our blessed union
Our happy homes

We became slaves to sex
Became slaves to our own lustful nature
We did not care how we got it as long as we got it

In all our doing God let us do it because we gave up our god for their god and it felt good to some
We did not care because we were not restricted to our nature – sexual desires
We kept on doing until we got sick and some even died
We cried out but our cries were in vain because we gave our God for someone else's own
We found out the hard way that their god could not cure us, heal us
We found out we were his slaves because we truly lost our own
We died – cried but in all we did we forgot the simple message in the fine prints the wages of sin is death but truth is life everlasting.

We defiled each other
Lay with each other
Fathers lying with daughters
Sisters lying with brothers
Brothers lying with sisters
Mothers lying with sons
Cousins lying with cousins
This was the norm of their society
A norm we learned because it became valuable to sell our own
It was the norm to be sinful and unholy
This was preached – taught hence it is still taught and preached until this day

We began to disrespect God
We brought filth in his holy places
We disgraced him while giving this new God our praise – thanks
We began to worship this new god even made idols – images onto him

We began to wear our shoes in the holy places of our God and became hated for this in them most vile of ways. We knew this was blatant disrespect but we did it anyway because this new god did not care. He gave us free reign to pollute and take from the land and we did without remorse or guilt.

Everything we had we began to lose but with all that we did not care we had free reign of the land. We became lawless – children without values – ambition – laws

We were cast out
We now had to find another way home
It was not pretty
There was no death in the garden
But because we tainted it
Polluted the land
We opened the door for death to rise
Sin to come in
We had to die because we now gave birth to sin so death came more and more

Death was now our new way home to God we were told but none remembered with our God – the God of Life – The True and Living God none had to die – none could die. We gave up life for death hence we die not to go to our home with our God but to go to home with their – this new god which is in hell.

We've faced many changes
There is many more to tell and come
Millions died
Billions more to come – die

We forgot about the cleanliness of God and made our bodies impure – unclean

We forgot about our colors the red, white and blue but truth be known the white, gold and green but in the highest form of spiritual life the white and blue – light blue – infinitely never ever dark blue. Dark blue belongs to the death – the powerful demons of hell but the truth is far from you our sisters, brothers, families of this earth.

We have our energy back
But we still have a long way to go
In making you overstand the concept of
Evolution
Creation
The Holy One – Good Life
The truth – true truth and real life of God

We still visit your planet in the forms of angels
Guardians
Masters
Teachers from time to time but we cannot stay hence the dreams come
Our way of communicating with you

Many have resorted to worshipping us
Calling us Gods but we are not Gods
We are God's creations
His instrument of home for the families we left behind

Over the centuries we have educated many messengers electing them to teach you in hopes that you too would find your way home to the Supreme One – The True and Living God

We gave them scrolls
Taught them to plant
Harvest from the land
Taught them the alignment of the planets
Planets when aligned would show them the way home

We even taught them to cure diseases
Heal the sick
Mummify the dead
We taught them how to create balance
Deal fairly with others
Everything we knew to be truthful and of life we taught them

We showed them how to build pyramids
Taught them how to build pyramids within pyramids

We used the pyramids vessels to find our underground world. We gave you the eye in the pyramid to let you know that the eye is the cubicle to life and death – the spiritual soul. There is more to the eye in the pyramid and eye but your knowledge of life is only based on the physical and not spiritual hence you cannot comprehend the eye in the pyramid and you will forever associate with demons – evil societies – wicked and evil people.

We see with our eyes but your spiritual eye sees further – greater because it is not limited to your space and time – world. The pyramid cannot be governed by the circle because the circle can be broken on the surface but cannot be broken when it is in the form of a dot.

As humans you know not of the dot
You know not of the eye in the triangle
You know not life
All you know is death hence you live to die and not live for life.

In our world we can manipulate and stop time

We can put simple messages in time for you to show you we still cared as well as waiting for you to return home

We even chose a selected few to tell humanity of the dangers of sin and the destruction that is to come which was set in time. Destruction caused by you humans because you continue on the pathway of sin and pure evil
We even taught these selected few - messengers how to use the sun moon and stars to tell time
How to use them as a gateway home
That was a challenge few could learn
A challenge you cannot see nor can you comprehend

It's simple really because all we teach is the truth but our language far exceeds the scope of your brain – mind. All you have to do is use your key – the passageway in your brain – the middle of your head to unlock all the doors leading to home but you must be clean – try to abstain from all sin. Also you cannot live inside the box because your box – your square is a prison. It cannot comprehend the knowledge of truth so it holds you prisoner inside it and refuse to set you free. You are its captive – the captive of the box but you have to break free of it and know the truth – LIVE.

My children how do I make you overstand
There is much to learn
How do I make you overstand your planet is dying
Shifting
Making way for your termination
Death
Extinction

How do I make you overstand and understand that earth – Mother Earth is dying? She has become death because you have all polluted her in the most abominable of ways.

How do I make you comprehend, overstand and understand that all you do in the name of sin you are taking away from your life.

How do I make you comprehend, overstand and understand that all the sins that you do – commit adds to the lake of fire on earth and this is why the earthquakes come, the severe storms come, the floods come, the severe rain comes – true death comes.

How do I make you overstand the importance of earth?

The importance of other planets as they are gateways to a new and different universe – life
Keys to a whole other universe
A universe a billion times more beautiful than this
A universe you never thought exist
A universe you cannot see in your polluted state of being - living

How do I get it through to you?

How do I tell you to stop the madness?
And return to the Supreme Being – God – Life
There are other beautiful planets and galaxies out there
Open your eyes
Your heart
Open your mind to peace – truth
It will lead you home if you try
Let us in – let the true and living God in
God will guide you to the truth
He will send his true and good guides to you to teach and educate you

We are here to help you
Let us help you to truly get home not in death but in LIFE

The rings are gone
Noah tried but you would not listen
Everyone was lost except for his family

Others have come but you would not listen - hear
You've tossed them aside like doormats
Cursed and abused them even killed them
This time will be different
Once we are gone
There will be no return
Your planet will be destroyed
Is slated for destruction and real soon

This solar system will no longer exist
The solar flames have been launched
It will take a few years to get there
Get to earth
But shortly
Less than twenty years
Chaos will rain on your planet – the planet earth

For a surety doom and gloom and humanity – the evil systems and wicked people of humanity will be totally destroyed

Here me my children
Stop the madness
And return – truly return home
Return to life – the True and Living God before it's too late.

Michelle

The five elements

There are four major elements
Air
Fire
Cold
Water
Earth

These are the five elements of man
Air we breathe – Cleans the inside- oxygen

Water – blood- replenishes – cleans

Fire – heat within our body to sustain and maintain life – clean

Cold – the moon to cool our bodies down

Earth – the body itself – houses the soul/spirit – which we must return – clean

All five work in unison
All five found on the planet earth
All five has one Supreme leader – ruler
All five need the sun and moon

There are many components we don't know
Like the supreme law of five and not four. Four represents the stage where evil came into being- the birth of negative forces – the North – Nod

For example there are four great rivers recorded by the ancients meaning according to man but in truth there are five if you count the Blue and White Nile
Four distinct races – Caucasians, Asians, Nubian, and Indian but in truth five if you count the mixture of races

Four entrances to the center of the earth but in truth five if you count the center and in truth no one can center the earth because over time due to evil the earth has lost its true center – space and place

Four corners to the planet earth – East, West, North and South but in fact the four corners of the earth represent the cross of evil – the square – the domain of all evil. The four degrees to a perfect square – 90, 90, 90, 90 = 360 which is your 6666 or your 24 – the time line of sin – all evil.

The square represents:
(Full circle – earth- the universe)
All degrees of the material world we reside in
Four degrees leading to **<u>one</u>** Supreme Being – Material – Evil
360 what we can see - physical

Basic knowledge leads to a greater knowledge – the truth.
The truth is within you
The truth and creation of the universe
The truth behind four - 24
You just have to find it – the truth
You must stay true to the truth
Be honest to it
Harness it
Grow in truth

Once the truth is altered it is no longer pure
No longer true
It becomes distorted
An infinite lie
It becomes sinful
Filthy
Unclean

It becomes like unto a dream
It becomes difficult to decipher – hard to read

Therefore it misleads causing you pain and a lot of grief
— sorrow

It leads to death of mind, body and spirit

Once the truth is altered it becomes of man and not of God because God gives the truth and man alter it

Once the truth is altered it becomes faded — washed out hence we live in anger
Stress
Frustration

And yes we infinitely die a greater death
A more painful death and that is the death of the spirit — the true you.

Michelle

A little fun

Enough of the sad talk
Doom and gloom
How are you?
Free your mind
Dust out the cobwebs

Smile, laugh a little
Let's play your favorite love song
Game
Grab your mate
Cuddle beside him – her
Take the remote

Let's play – here we go
Miss Whitney – You bring good love
Prince – Diamonds and Pearls

No don't want to go there
Let's go here and have some fun

Hope these will light up your face
So come on lets have some fun
Here we go:

God I am going to bug you today
Drive you crazy
Gonna pinch you
Be like a child – a big baby
I'll even annoy you
Because that's what friends do at times
And you are the bestest friend I've ever had

I can come to you with my problems

Come to you with my sorrows
My joys and laughter
And I know my problems will stay with you
My problems will not be broadcasted over the six o'clock news no wait instagrammed

I know that in time you will assist me
Comfort me
Make my troubles go away
So yes I am going to bug you
Hug you, kiss you
Treat you like my pet – my chia pet that grows because I give good care – true and infinite love

Yes the treatment is good and pure because you are pure and good and you are infinitely dear to me

Michelle/MJ

Father God, am I getting through to you yet?
Do you have a smile on your face?
When I write and think these things
Truly think of you and having fun with you

People must think me crazy for loving you so much
Think me crazy for writing and thinking the way I do
But I don't care as I am playful at heart
Cause boy do I truly love you
The things I do to you
Only Michelle can do

I know you have the heart of a lion
Strong, pure, patient, full of love
And to put up with me you need these qualities – the heart of a lion. You have to be strong and infinitely patient because I will put you to the test and you know I do

At times we are at odds
Well I'm at odds with you
And at times I picture you smiling
Saying "child I don't know what to do with you but I do truly love you."

For those times I drive you crazy
Like now
I do hope it makes you happy and put a beautiful and everlasting smile upon your face

God you know me

Love always and forever my gorgeous and beautiful king – true love always infinitely.

Michelle

Okay, okay I take it you don't like those.

Well how about these. Ladies when you see that fine buck of a man that you just want to share your bed forever with. That fine buck that has swept you off your feet and you get so infatuated with that person that all you can see is him. You want to tell him or her how you feel but you don't know how to do so. Well hope these little nudges help to soothe your senses.

Ode to the men I am infatuated with based on looks alone not deeds. Shaq don't get jealous because you are infinite play in my books. Don't know why I infinitely like to play with you. Maybe it's because you are tall, handsome and so so black – yes you are a brother okay. And people my play is not limited to the brothers okay. I have my fun and you have your fun so appease me – yes oblige me okay it's not every day I have a little fun and play.

Do hope your significant others don't mind as well as hope you get a chuckle out of my dedication to all of you as this was done in fun; fun of going wild my thoughts. So George, Mikhail, Dean, Tyrese, Djimon, Fantan, Queen Latifah, do not take me seriously well Dean and Mikhail you can. Just kidding it's all in fun people.

MJ/Michelle

Ah the beauty of my African Queen
Beautiful you are to me
Gorgeous in all your glory

You are just right
Big, bold – entertaining
You are a voluptuous flower
My yellow rose

Ah my black beauty
Beautiful African Queen
Thank you my darling for representing
You are a rare and precious queen
Black onyx, black gold

You are a true African Queen and I truly love you

Michelle

My Queen be proud of you
You are talented – funny

You are private – the corner rose
You are black woman – black beauty

You are strong
An ancient flower
You are queen
Queen Latifah

Michelle

Baby I am going crazy for you
Can't fight these feelings anymore
I feel like I am going to loose my mind
I can't touch or feel you
But I so desire you

Your picture I keep in my heart
If only you could unlock the feelings to these doors
Give me the keys to your heart
And stop me from going crazy
Overboard

Your picture I have posted on my wall
Pictures I look at each and every day
Pictures I've had to take down
Lest I die with love for you

Baby you're all I think about
I am sick with love – death
Don't know what to do
Wish I could be the key to your heart
The rose you see each and every morning – each and every day
I wish I could be the sun that rises and sets on you
In you

Oh if only I could be the corn that grows in your garden
The sheet that outlines your bed
The sparkle that lights up your eyes

In my eyes you are perfect
I wish I could get with you
Baby for now I surrender to you in my heart
But one day
One day I hope I will become your angel
Your queen in paradise
Your one in love
Your all and all

MICHELLE

Oh baby when I see your face my world fall to pieces – melts me to the ground
The smile that encompass my face
The love I think of making to you as you surrender to me

Oh baby blue blow your saxophone for me
Let your music devour me – entangle me
The songs you sing – play they keep me coming back crying for more
Baby play for me
Let my world be your instrument of joy – play
Ah yes simply breath taking – paradise

Ah Dean play for me butterfly for me
It's the feel I get when I think of you
It's my anthem – our anthem – butterfly that is so
Thank you for expressing it so nicely

I know for now this is just a passing fancy – musical fantasy
As you have replaced Shaq
Well not yet
He's still the perfect friend in lala land in my book
You are my musical genius and forever will be in my book

Yes I am naughty but will give up Shaq for one night just to have you play the blues for me. Sorry Shaq but have you seen this man play? He's that good better than his peers.
Mama Blue respect is due. You are his queen and I have to infinitely respect you. I do hope you understand. This is my way of fun – musical fun that's clean musically. There is infinitely no cheating because that is simply nasty – not fun

So Mama Blue across the miles respect is truly due
It is given with the highest of honor so please see with me

But with all that aside
You know the truth
As I don't believe in lies

One day my fantasy
One day you will be mine
All my desires will take fold
Hope you are up to it
Hope the naughtiness comes out in you
Because I know it will come out in me musically.

MJ

PS for all that think otherwise take your mind out of the gutter especially my words in the end. It is a musical one night stand that I am talking about. No ooh's respect is due to wifey and family.

Michelle

My mind is free
Hope yours is too
We can do more than meet down by the river

We can start a fire
Not a bon fire
But lovers caught up in the heat of the moment
Lovers letting our natural juices flow

I will touch your body like no other
Forget about my fingers
Tongue
But let the sweetness of my breath take fold
Spread through your body down to your loins
As I take you to paradise in the heat of the day
The heat of loves wonderful bliss – fire

Come on Mikhail let me introduce you to my world
Forget about Shaq he won't mind
Forget about all my other infatuations
Come on take my hand
And come into my world

A world filled with passion
A world filled with love

An hour just won't do
We will go all day
All night if you please

Come on Mikhail let me introduce you to my world
A world filled with passion
A world filled with love
I promise you

Give you my word
I will not hurt you

So come on Mikhail take my hand and let me introduce in to my world
A world of love – truth
A world situated in heaven – God's true paradise.

Michelle

My darling the feathers of God's beauty surround me

The coolness of your skin makes me want to devour you

White chocolate so sweet
Good for the heart
Good for the soul
Soul food

Baby for just one night if not a lifetime
Let me do you right – do right by you
Let me into your world
Let me complete you

There are no games here
No lies on my part
No lies of the heart
Only truth – true love – infatuation
Let's take the world by storm
Make beautiful music together
Write music-music that is heaven sent
Eternal

We can write love songs to comfort
Make love to

Forget about the office or the bedroom
We can write by the oasis of God – that which he has given me

On those lazy days we will throw ideas at each other, political ideas, sports ideas – football though.

Sorry Shaq you know how I feel about basketball.
Give me football over basket ball any day.

Yes the lonely nights of laying arm in arm in our hammock
The bed will do too
Ah yes the floor

Baby, take a load off
Free your mind
Ascend to paradise with me
Not on chariots – as they depict war
But on the clouds wrapped in each other's loving arms

My Darling, join with me
I will be yours completely
I will complete thee – you
I will bring back your youth
Give you true joy
I will give you true love because true love resides in me.

MJ

My Samson, wrap your long dreadlocks around me
Shield my breasts with thy long dark hair
Let me bask in your heavenly glory
Feel the strength of your haven – hair
Come on baby forget about Delilah
There is no Delilah here
I will never deceive you nor take advantage of you
Nor will I cut your hair

I will be your queen
You my king
I will rub your head
Drive away your pain
I will soothe your aching feet with the purest of aloe
that which is my loving touch – tender caress
I will make you your favorite drink
Will set your bath with the oils of heaven
Oils to ease your mind
Oils that will take away your sorrows
Oils that will relax you
Truly comfort you

My Samson, My King
Wrap your long dark lox around me
Shield me from the darkness of this world
Bring me peace within

Spread your long dread lox upon my chest
Let me dry it like the sun
Let me bask in it
Like the angels of heaven basking in God's sweet sweet honey – Aloe

My Samson you are the one
Be my king
And I will be your queen

I will never deceive you
Lie to you or hurt you

Take my hand like a child holding the hand of God
Take my hand like a saint holding on to God
Trust is the key
True love the conqueror of all

Take my hand and let me in
Let the blessing of God engulf us
Surround us
My Samson my hand is extended
Will you take it and be eternally true
Eternally true to you and me
My love a yes is all it takes because in my eyes a yes is true
It is honest
Can never lie
So take my hand it is extended in truth to thee – you

Michelle

What is this feeling I have for you?
Why can't I get you out of my head?
Daily I fanaticize about you
Being your wife
Your lover
Your all

Yes I see the outside
You are good looking
The one I want
But unfortunately I do not know your insides
What you stand for
What you are all about

Yes I can ask a million and one questions
But does that make me truly know you
Yes you have the body that I want
Your face is handsome
And I can't get enough of you

Yes I would love to get to know you
I would like to share a blessed life with you
A union based on true love – trust
A union based on truth
A union ordained by God
Blessed by God for all eternity

Man oh man how the world would envy us
Because the union would be truly blessed

Truly sanctified by God – Divine

But yet I can only wonder
Ponder what life would be like with you
I do hope one day the two will meet
On that day I truly hope God will bless us
Make and consecrate a perfect union with one true mate.

A true and honest mate

A truthful mate sent by God – the True and Living God

So sorry George, Queen Latifah, Fantan, Dean and Mikhail because God takes precedence in my book and you're all just my passing fantasies – my secret well not so secret fantasies.

Michelle

Man do you ever look fine
Damn boy you are good looking
Muscular
Thick as a whip
Sexy as a flower

Wow if I could have you forever
My mind is racing
As to the things I would love to do to you

If only I could eat you like a chocoholic relishing in the sweetness of fine chocolate
If only I could explore you like a seasoned explorer
I would navigate you to my world
A world of pure sunshine - pleasure

Wow I better stop
Because whip cream is on my mind
A taste of honey just won't do
Want to peel you like a professional peeling the skin off a Jackfruit
Yeah a chef peeling a banana
Don't worry baby you can core me any day
Trust me I will be your apple no forget apples are associated with Eve – sin so scrap that – those thoughts of sin but in truth the apple resembles the heart – the human heart hence it is depicted and used in the bible.

But don't worry I will take tender care
No roughness here
But if you are into the rough stuff
Trust me I can play too as long as I take charge – the lead
But just for you I will take my time
So you can feel the electricity flowing in my fingers – pulsating through my veins as electrical currents targets your loins
Electric flow that heats up your body
And make you stand still – at will

Baby let my current move you – fool you
No not fool you intoxicate you like fine wine nudging your senses

Let it take control of you like hard liquor talking to you

Make you walk beyond the clouds

(Sorry people because I know some are trying hard to stay clean so please forgive me for saying hard liquor and please do not take it personal). For you that are going to protest I will not take this line out to please you or anyone.

It won't take a minute or two
Whatever your hearts desire I will give to you

Man do you ever look fine
A mango has nothing on you
Come on let me urge you
Take the plunge
Let me satisfy you

Michelle

Baby I don't want to see your pictures no more
Wanna see you
Touch you
Kiss you

Trust me I would be glued to you
Enjoying you
Even if it's just for a moment or two

You are sexy
My perfect mate
Hair long and perfect
Neatly twisted – loxed

Ya, I can play in it all day
Even twist the hair on your chest

I can see your muscled arms around me
Molding me in your loving arms
We can talk all night
Tell a joke or two

Baby you are a fine brother
Yes I am infatuated with you
My only hope is that your inner
Is as beautiful as the outer

Do hope you are kind, generous and thoughtful
If not:
Sayonara
Don't want to get to know you
Or be with you no more

Michelle

Touch my lips
Enjoy it like fine wine
Engulf me with your flame
Enrich my heart with your love of truth
Serenade me with honesty
Serenade me with life – truth

Be the tile outlining my floor
My Benz that is carefully driven
My exotic juices
Exotic fruits
Sweet to the taste
Smooth going down

My darling
Touch my lips
Engulf me with your flame
Fire desired by lovers
Fire that burns like lava
Fire that consumes

My darling
Take this rose
Kiss it
Let us become one unified in heart – desire
One union in love – the love of truth
One union at heart – good and true pleasure

Michelle

I can feel the warmth in your hand
Touch so soft it makes my body tingles
A softness that makes us become as one
Unify as one

The desire within me
The desire within you
Love that light up heaven above

No one can make me feel as you do
No one that can render me helpless at a mere touch as you do

My darling and love
Tonight I surrender to you completely
Give you my love
In love
Because all I see is true love within you

Michelle

Another day has come and gone and boredom looms. Nothing to do but play video games

Man what a day

Sometimes I want to go out but can't – too cold
Body cannot function in the cold. Need sunshine the Jamaican sunshine – homeland.

Miss Jamaica much hence I feel trapped here inside the cold

Need me my black, sexy dark skinned chocolate of a man to cool me down in the land of the sun

Oh yea I was talking about the cold

Ladies can you imagine biting in that dark black hunk of a man

Ah yes blackberries sweeter than cherries
Sweeter than fine wine
The most expensive dark chocolate

Ah my fine black man skin blacker than tonic
Heaven sent – blessed

Yea baby give me my fine black chocolate any day any time

Finely roasted
Filled with minerals – the finest of ores –onyx, bdellium, crystal – fine black crystal – black gold.

Yes you are cherished – divine
Yes my black chocolate – black man in all your glory you are without form and void – genesis
Oh man honey – my sweet and fine black man
God did a magnificent job when he created you

You are perfect more than fine

You are rare – rarest of diamonds

My back man just look at you glory divine

Skin smooth as silk
Tattoo free
You are truly heavenly and I am blessed to call you mine – say you are mine mine mine

Michelle

Black man pow –
Yes wow

Black man be my jungle

Ride me like
Like a stallion journeying home

Take my lust of you to new heights – heaven

Let me gaze and graze upon thy beauty. Honey let me look at you, touch your black chocolate skin cause honey your skin is magnificent – divine

Baby you are my black chocolate
Come let me ravish you
Taste your chocolate divine – skin

Just stand there for me.
Naked as you are because baby the old adage is right the blacker the berry the sweeter the juice but in your case the ride

Yes my black man take pride in your heavenly ride – skin. You are perfect and I am infinitely proud of you – your black skin.

Michelle

Hey my black brother let me lay on your skin.
Let me touch it, feel it – get lost in it

Hey my black brother won't you join me
Soothe me
Let me drink of the juices of your fine black skin – chocolate

Let me melt you
Consume you
Find favour in you

Ah my brother, tease me with your black beauty
I am woman
A fine black woman
Your black queen

I am bold
Daring
Charming
Truly loving

Won't you be my black king – everything
Everything of me I will give to you

Everything of me I will teach you. Just take my hand and let me bask in your fine dark skin – black skin

Let me cherish you because your skin is of God
Truly beautiful – pure – real
Hey my black brother, take my hand. Let's be free as I take note and cherish you – cherish your fine black skin.

Michelle

To all my black brothers out there that does not have a tattoo. You are blessed and highly favored by God and I so truly and infinitely love you.

You are representing God
You are true to him – true to you

You are one of God's own and for this respect is due

God loves you because you are not a part of the devil's clan. Props to you – props to God and thank you for respecting him – God.

To all of you my black brothers. Truly thank you for respecting God and the beautiful natural black skin he has given you.

Michelle

Heaven's gate is open wide
Receive your blessings my black kings.
Receive your blessings because you are true to your skin
You are true to God and you did not defile him.
You don't bleach your skin
You respect God and the black beauty he has infinitely given you.

Michelle

My Darling how I love to look upon you
Your skin drives me crazy all the time

Look at you you fine black man you
Ah baby if only I could eat you – devour you
Man if only I could chew upon your black onyx skin

My black man a diamond has nothing on you because you are priceless – rare

Ah man, I want to chew you, lick you, eat you, squeeze you – your skin.

My black man can I have your skin. Ah baby just let me look at you again and again. You are God's creation because you be fineeeeeeeeeeeeeeeeeeeeee. Man the beauty of infinity does not compare to you. God please don't get jealous but have you looked upon the black man's skin lately.

God you did me proud – heavenly
Better tomorrow. No baby the black man's skin is my better tomorrow. God look at Djimon Hounsou. Lovely with his fine and delicious black skin. He is black beauty. God with skin like his who needs honey. God he's fine molasses …..you know what I better stop.

God thank you for making perfect and beautiful skin like Djimon Hounsou.

Michelle

Do hope you enjoyed the poems above. As you can see infatuation is one hell of a thing. It can take you to another world and back. It can make you think of some ungodly things. Hence:

Outer appearance is deadly
Everything we do is based on looks
Vanity

How easy is it to be misguided?
Mislead

What is unfortunate or disheartening is that we do not look at the inner – the heart
We do not read the person's aura
Concede to what our heart is saying
Beauty – outer appearance is all to many hence vanity, the search for perfection – ultimate beauty.

Ladies know that for many the inside is fowl
For others it's like a raisin that has been baked by the sun – in the sun
Wrinkly but sweet as hell
Filled with vitamin D, Antioxidants
A brown to black or purple hue that makes you want to chew all night and never let go
The juice is so fine it keeps you coming back for more

It has natural sugars and regulates you like a prune

It doesn't go sour or stale
It's in its natural state
It's good for you
Regulate your system
Digestive tract
But yet men cannot see the prune or the raisin in you

They see only the grape – a sour grape
When they bite into it
Aaaaah is it ever sour
So sour you have to squeeze your eyes shut – close

That's why it's good to stay with the raisin you have because in truth raisins are never sour
They are always sweet
Yes as sweet as me and you but a little wrinkly.

Michelle

Do hope you are enjoying thus far. These next set of poems are for lovers in love. It does not matter the age. You could be ninety six and still be in love. Enjoy and have fun. Michelle

My Darling
My Love
Let's paint the town no not downtown
Let's take a stroll down memory lane
Have a walk in the park
Skip to my Lou

Holding hands just won't do
Let's make our own little history
Based on truth, love and pure harmony

Let's kiss all our troubles away
Make love in the park
Under the moonlight
Under the bed
Ah yes in the bathtub
Atop the roof
In the bushes
In the kitchen
Along the sea

Let's make the angels sing
Laugh and giggle

Let's become true friends once again

We will erase the past of all bad memories
Erase the past of all our pain
Erase it of war
The deceitful things we use to do
The wrongs of my ancestors
The wrongs of all future generations

Let's make a new world
Based on solid and pure trust – infinite trust
Solid and pure infinite love

Let's put nothing negative there
All that must be there is:
Positive love
Positive vibrations
Positive humanity
All that is positive
All that is positive in you
You
All that is infinitely good

Michelle

My Collective – The Dark Side of Me – Part One

Let me touch your face tenderly
Let me reside with you
Let me hold you
Mould you in my body
Wrap you in my tender and loving arms

Let's sit by the fire
Sipping pure and natural cocoa
Dining on cucumber sandwiches
An ice cream bar or two

No music will play
We will make our own
This will be our time together
Time spent between me and you

The children are in bed
Fast asleep
Let's make our own beautiful music
Just you and me beside the fire

We don't have to make love
We can just lay there in each others arms
You telling me of your day
And me telling you just how much I truly love you
Cause you know I do

Tonight and forever let it be me and you
If not by the fire
In the bath
On the bed

Even on the floor
Whatever our hearts desire
You and I
Me and you
We'll do it all together in truth and harmony

Michelle

Dean Fraser, play for me
Blown your horn like lovers entwined
Two lover's in love
Discovering each other for the first time

Let your music take me to a different world
Let it be like sweet wine to my soul
Let your music touch me
Bathe me
Warm me

Let it pluck me
Mould me
Wrap me up forever in love infinitely

Come on Dean thrill me with your love
Let your Sax
Your horn bring heaven from above

Come on be my angel upon the horn
Play for me
Come on baby play
Play like you've never played before
Play for me like a harpist in tune with his harp
Come on Dean
Mr. Fraser
Take me to your world and back
Write your music in my heart
Let it make me float in your cocoon of love
Respect

Michelle

"Come on baby lets go."

"Go where?"

"Down by the river."

"Why don't we just play the song, Morgan Heritage will do. They sing down by the river."

"You know what forget it. I will go by myself." He laughs at her as he did not see nor hear the seriousness in her tone the upset look on her face.

"You think I am funny. A woman want to be romantic, go down to the river and bathe her man, wash his nappy ass hair, make him feel good, show the world she truly loves him, care about him and you laugh at me."

"Girl that shit ain't romantic. We have a bedroom. That's what it's there for. We have the sofa, shit we even have the floor."

"So that's it, you don't want to do any of this". She said exasperatedly. She had wanted to get through to him but her mind told her otherwise. She had to try another approach. "Alright, let's go outside under the moonlight. You and me together having nothing but pure adult triple X rated sex as two bodies unified as one, infused in passion. We will become one desire as we touch each other, exploring each other as the rays of the moon and stars bless us and shower us with its love."

"You know what you are whack. There are people outside, nosy neighbors. Besides don't want to get my skin or hair dirty."

"So everything I want we can't do."

"No, they are not romantic to me", he said boldly. "Thank you because now I know you don't truly love me".

"Baby I love you but not in your kinky way. I am home grown and not into the extended foreplay or boring shit like taking a walk, cuddling. We have each other we don't need the mushy shit".

The stage was set. All she wanted she could not find in him. Leaving him she waited and waited for the right one to come along. The right one that would have an opened mind, inclined to do all she wanted to do and more. The right someone that would take long walks with her even hold her hand.

It was not easy for her and just when she was ready to give up God answered her prayer. Mr. Right, Mr. Perfect came knocking at her door no not the mail man but the repair man. She had the man of her dreams now the one with the fine dreadlocks and good heart, a man that loved her and was not afraid to hold her hand or try new things. Now from time to time she took her man to the river and bathes him even made love to him under the moonlight. All she wanted in a man she got in him and yes they lived happily because she had found her one true king, Mr. Right, Mr. Perfect, Mr. Blessed because God did send her the right man. Time now told, hearts beat in unison, angels sing – glory divine because divine love did come – came. She did retreat; she did enjoy and kept true to the man God had given her.

MICHELLE

Okay my love what are we going to do today
I know I have to walk to the grocery store and get a couple of things
Walking is my in thing – the in thing
A brisk walk not no lazy walk – thing

Thank you for providing me with the running shoes too now I hope the circulation in my body improves. I also hope it will start healing itself and stop decaying

Need to burn off some of this fat
Don`t need anymore complications and all that
Need to keep holding on to you
Need you to take charge of my life – my family
My health
My inner organs
Everything

Man cannot fix me but I know you can
I am not just relying on you
I am counting on you
Hoping on you
Have faith in you
Trust you
Because I know you will heal me
Because you truly love me

Michelle

I am weathering the storm no matter how hard it rages

I am going through the fire no matter how hot it blazes

In the end I know you will be there with me

I know you are in the storm and fire with me

You could have let me go long ago but you never gave up on me instead you stayed with me

You knew I would turn back my love to you and yes drive you crazy

The relationship we have I need it to grow further

I don`t know but right now I truly need you as a friend

Someone to talk to and although we have that I need to see you

Please do not hide your face from me

I need you to stand beside me

Helping me to make all the decisions I need to make

I know I ask a lot and will always ask a lot but that's just me. I need you in my life. I need all the goodness you can offer me. I need your strength and your true love.

My Collective – The Dark Side of Me – Part One

Father, my love, confidant, friend wrap me in your loving arms in a good and divine way

Hold me securely from behind and nestle my head in your chest

Tell me you truly love me and need me in your life

Tell me I am important to you and that you will infinitely never let me go or leave me

Tell me you truly care about me like I truly love and care about you

Tell me you will always protect me and my family from all evil – truly

My Love always let me feel truly cared for and truly loved

Eternal Father, tell me that you are truly there for me and yes I omitted the Darling because I am so mad at you.

Today I need you to prove yourself to me because in all that I see and know you are not truly there for me. All I see is women. I have never truly received a good gift from a man. When I said I needed you to hold me the one that came was a woman. She held me in the kitchen and did not let me go. So my mind is baffling as I assess the ages and all that I see because all that I see are women being good to me. If I see a male they lead me into danger and I would be the one having to have to get out of it. I am left alone to conquer my demons – obstacles alone. Even the sword of death – that sword that kills

Satan – evil that was taken from me by my own black man yes he said he loved me but you know what God there is love and then there is true love and the greatest gift any human can have is true love because it is pure, truthful – truly forgiving. True love does not hold a grudge and true love cannot abandon their children. We all make mistakes and have faults but you cannot give up on your own because we all make mistakes even you God. Yes Eve sinned like I did and still do but you know what God as a father you could have corrected her and tell her she was wrong but instead you kicked her out of your abode never to return. God I've told you you are a lousy teacher because your language is different from man. If we do not know something you cannot hold us guilty of sin nor can you expect us to figure it out when we do not know where to look. You did the same thing to me and I fell victim of sin and yes I paid the price and penalty because once you marry a dirty – sinful man your life is over because that dirty man does everything in his power to tie you to him and make you fail, make you die at his hands. He is not clean because he does cheat on you, stress you out to the point where you want to kill yourself, he abuses you, beats you to a pulp this I know because I know the true hands of evil. Evil beats you into submission hence in my book man cannot be good but pure evil. None that I see on the face of this earth is good and for this I am waiting for you to prove me wrong. All I see in man is evil – vanity – greed – lust all that is bad. You God cannot see true goodness because at times I don't think truth reside in you. Yes I am entitled to my views hence I come to you and tell you how I feel. This earth is run by greedy and wicked men because all the do is store up and do not truly see the needs of the poor – needy hence in their books of sin that they write to deceive and lead nations to hell it said "to have dominion over the land and subdue it" so when you have dominion over the land you have dominion over humans not just the animals and you kill to keep dominion – control and this is what man do because they say this is from you. So tell me God what makes you good? What makes you Life? What makes you the true and living God? When it's all said and done are you not like man because you are male? Are you not wicked apart of the wicked clan – man?

And in the book of sin it said and God made man in his own image – in the image of God created he them male and female. And female is another type of male. You know that and I know that but it does not give us the right to disrespect or mistreat each other because in your true state there is no gender and no one on the face of the planet can tell me or you what you truly look like – hence energy. Yes you show us you in the form that our mind and eyes can see you and even in doing do you are wrong because this is not the true you.

Hence with you God I infinitely trust you but it does not mean you are to take disadvantage of my trust and truth of you. I do not do it to you so please do not do it to me. I know I have to learn certain things but in truth God I am tired of evil and the evil that men do. Yes I know your position but to be honest with you those that are true to you be true to them because we did not ask to come into this sinful world. I infinitely did not hence sometimes I am at odds with you because I want and need better not just for the earth but for you good people that is in the earth as well as a part of the human race. I've excluded the spiritual race because I know you have your good people in the spiritual with you already. I know the change hence I know the triangle and what it represents. I infinitely love you and care about you but you have to do the same meaning make me feel loved – truly a part of you. I cannot argue with you anymore because I am infinitely tired of it – tired of the evil of this earth. I am not happy and you cannot keep me living in sin if sin is infinitely hurting me. This is wrong. You call us to you then leave us to die in filth come on now. We are not filth we are your children and as a father your job is to provide for us and keep us safe. You cannot abandon us and be like the human sperm donors of this land – earth. God I know you hence I can come to you with everything so people if you do not know God infinitely do not do what I do because like I said there is infinite trust and truth and true love between me and God and when I am angry I take out my frustrations on him. You can do the same but you have to have a true relationship with God. And yes for those who are saying I bet you don't do this with your children I do. I cuss them out when they are wrong and I tell them if I am wrong to tell me. Never lie to me because when you lie to me I will go off – get upset. Like I've said and will forever say your relationship with God is yours and no one has a right to tell you how to have it. God does not do it so man should not do it. Always infinitely always go to God with truth because God seeks the truth from man not lies. Evil loves lies hence he has us lying and when evil does this he keeps us away from God and no one should hinder anyone from getting to God or having a good and clean yes honest relationship with him.

God regardless of what we do, you are still our father. I agree that there are certain things you cannot put up with because as humans we don't put up with certain things in life like filth – a dirty and unclean place. I can't stand it because it makes me cross. This I give you plus some more.

Yes I know sin is nasty and loves nastiness hence sin keeps us sinning and living in his nasty world – nastiness. Been there done that because one cannot be clean and the other dirty this I know. Yes I know if you lay with a nasty man your surroundings will become dirty and it's a hell of a thing to get rid of or out of that nasty home or apartment. This I can testify to. Hence people I tell you know the colors of truth – God because if you don't you will be doomed.

There are essential colors and you need to know them because colors affect your world – the living. I can't figure out darkness yet meaning nighttime and when I do I will let you know. If you can tell me what it means using a flashlight in the night and the flashlight suddenly die let me know because I can't figure that one out. No in my night dream it is not pitch black there is always light – moonlight or nightlight to guide me. I am never in total darkness for those who want elaboration. Oh man this reminds me of Daniel. No I am not the king though. Smile.

Michelle

Ode to Robert Nesta Marley
From Natural Mystic to Chances Are
From Trench Town to the World
No one truly knew who you were
A poet in your own right
A musical icon, legend and king

You stand and surpass all the others before you
You stand as a king
Ride in the boat of Solomon and the likes of him
Your heritage was the same as him
Your music foretold your wisdom
Words that are powerful
Words that told the truth
Words that made you a reggae king
A Jamaican idol
A Jamaican king

Flamboyant and dashing you were
I can only imagine what you would be like today
If you weren't taken away suddenly

I see your reign
One carefully bred
Your seed
Only one can and will carry on
Will wear your crown

His musical talent
One I admire
I can only hope he can live up to your Royal name
Your heritage
Your place as king – reggae king
Bobby you were a genius
You stand in the rank of
Prince
Hendrix
Beethoven
But there is only one
And that one is you
Bob Marley
The King – Reggae King

And although many will try they cannot duplicate you. None can say they are incarnated of you because as old people say duppy noa who fi frighten.

No one can take your place because your name has meaning hence in the spiritual realm you are not called Robert Nesta Marley or Bob Marley you are called King Charo. No one knows this but I do.

No one can take the place of a lion you and I know this, hence fools will talk and mimic hence it is fools that thread on lands they know nothing about. Death cannot walk the lands of the righteous and it is fools that follow the blind man that cannot see the light of day nor can he see the light in the dark and what's waiting for him at the end of the road.

Bob you were an inspirational messenger
Musical legend – genius
True peace be with you always my brother because where you are you are at rest with the ancients – the ancient Rasta Mans. For those who know – know. For others they cannot comprehend and will never comprehend because they know not the power and purity – the legend of the Rasta man's hair – kingdom.

Michelle

Bobby you came
You sang
Delivered your message of truth
You did God's bidding
You gave the world you
Then you went away
Leaving the world to mourn your loss
Leaving the world to mourn you

You left that space
That space for someone to come and tell the world
Open the eyes of the world to your message
The message of truth
The message of God
That Natural Mystic
You

You are timeless and your music will live on forever – from generation to generation
We will speak of you – Bob Marley
When you spoke of a Natural Mystic in the air no one understood you. They did not understand that they could hear and feel God if they took the time to listen and be quiet

Ambush in the night
You were telling them of the plots against you
Telling your people not to listen to the lies pagans – Babylonians – the clergy
You told them not to listen to the politician's and their scams because they will deceive you and leave you begging in the streets like dogs begging for bread
You told us they will trick you
Then turn against you
Kill you

You told your people to open their eyes
To a better way of life
A peaceful way of life
Truth
You also told them not to get caught up in the system. A system that feeds you lies
Rape you of their dignity – self worth
A system that robs you of their spirituality
A system that keeps you ignorant – enslaved
A system that keeps you begging
A system that robs you of your prosperity – land – home

You spoke of your death in Chances Are
Told your people and the world

Foretold of the death of some of your band members

You told them they would not make it but they could not comprehend this. They too did not listen

You gave your life for your people
But still they would not listen
Could not comprehend your message

Today they deem you as a musical legend and king
Yet they still cannot see – do not know
You have opened the door to a better way of thinking
A better way of doing things
A better way of life
And still they cannot see the message you gave to them
The education you taught them like Marcus Mosiah Garvey before you

Like other messengers before you
You came from rags to riches
To show your people and the world
The way to a life of peace – true love
Your music was all you had
That was your way
The gift that God gave you

Now your music and message will live on for future generations for more than a thousand life times
My only hope now is that as my generation gets older
They will fully understand and overstand the truth
Teach their children of the truth
Use your music as a tool to aide them to spread truth and true love in a good way
The way God taught you
The way it was truly meant to be

Michelle

Many have come and gone
But none can live in the hearts as the chosen few
Marcus Mosiah Garvey
Robert Nesta Marley
Paul Bogle
Nanny
Solomon
Moses
Noah
Nelson Mandela
Ruth
Daniel
Just to name a few
Each had a job to do and they did it
You were no exception

My musical genius the legacy you left behind is unparallel to none
You were in your own class
Your own rank because God gave you music to teach – heal – soothe

No one can tell me you were not one of the chosen few

No one can deny you your place with God
No one can deny the herb
It does heal you like the aloe
Cleanse you
Calms your soul because it burns strong
Takes away your pain
Opens your eyes meaning heal your eyes
It is as unique as you

It takes away your fears
Mellows you out

My Collective – The Dark Side of Me – Part One

Like you've said time and time again
What they don't understand people will go against
Destroy like they did you
Even turn from you

But they did not understand you
They still don't
But in time my musical messenger
My musical icon, genius and legend – musical king
In time they will understand you
The message you brought and delivered

Peace must reign again
The righteous will stand
Because when I hear songs like:

Rise Again	*Duane Stephenson*
Truth Is	*Duane Stephenson*
Tell me how come	*Morgan Heritage*
Jealousy	*Morgan Heritage*
Corruption	*Fantan Mojah*
Hungry	*Fantan Mojah*
Poverty	*Cocoa Tea*
Holy Mount Zion	*Cocoa Tea*
Roots	*Etana*
Bad Man Chill Out	*Alborosie*
Free Yourself	*Alborosie*
Same Gun	*QQ*
One Day	*Matisyahu*
One Stone	*Culture*
Down in Jamaica	*Culture*
Can't Walk	*Mr. Vegas, Ghost+*
Tek Wey Yuself	*Mr. Vegas*
Sweet Jamaica	*Shaggy, Mr. Vegas+*
Rastafari Is	*Peter Tosh*
Marcus Garvey	*Tarrus Riley*

Black Mother Pray   Tarrus Riley

Special note and recognition to Mutabaruka, Burning Spear and Yellowman they also paved the way for us to learn and trod on no matter our trials and tribulations. Everyone in the industry should take a note as well as a page out of Yellowman's book. He was diagnosed with Cancer and through his ordeal he still persevered. He never gave up because he is still trodding along on the reggae musical train

I know that very soon your people and country will be okay – rise again and break the chains of mental and physical slavery, political oppression and political genocide. I know we will repent and put away all manner of evil, killing, strife, self hate, rudeness, sexual lust – gratification – multiple partners

Despite the adversity and hardship they face I know we will rise again in a good and prosperous manner –way because when I see the works of Shaggy and what he is doing for the Bustamante Children's Hospital I am filled with hope and pride. Hope and Pride because your words is not going in vain. Someone is truly listening - carrying on in a good way – in their own way. I have to truly give God thanks for him (Shaggy) because he is doing what no other artists can. God has blessed them with good fortune and instead of coming together to help Jamaica in a good and positive way they wage war and strife amongst each other. None can truly give hence in the end of life they will not be truly blessed. They will be shun by God because all have life and could not give to life in a true and giving way. Shaggy is truly giving back in his way and I ask God to truly bless him and the good works he is doing. He's set the bar Bobby, he's set the bar. I know Bobby I know because Shaggy is truly blessed because he is not only giving back in a good way to his people – children – the children of Bustamante Hospital but he is also giving back to God in a good and precious way.

One day Bobby one day. Yes the earth – people of this earth will mourn because you did say many more will have to suffer and many more will have to die don't ask me why. You knew what was to come this I know because I do comprehend and I do listen. But as I wait I know one day every Jamaican will see the beauty of Jamaica and walk in life therefore giving Jamaica new life – hope. One day Bob Jamaica will have the true life of God again and God will truly walk with his people the way it was meant to be. We will rise in the goodness of God and no one will make us stray again or deceive God and self.

I know Chances Are is not in vain and that one day Jamaican and the like will once again return home to The Most High God – The True and Ever Living God.

I've seen your abode and know the mountain and as long as I live I will carry on and will never forget your good words – hope, true love – true trust.

Michelle

To you my musical king
Your music
Your words and music must live on in the hearts of the chosen few
Your words and music must live on in the hearts of the world

Your music must be a testament
An eternal plea to the wicked
The unjust – wicked at heart

One day my musical king
There will be an Exodus
Jah's people must return home
Return to Ja-mai-ca the land and lands where God made them

Like you've said:
No matter how they kill us
Many more will come
Many more will rise
And the world will take notice of God – Jah
Ja-Mai-Ca

The way of true peace and true love is correct – exact and cannot change
Truly loving thy neighbor
Showing true love
That warm embrace
Being truthful to one's self – one another
What you believe in – know to be true
The true love of God is the key to opening all doors
The true love of all
Humanity
But yet many say they love but have not love – are not true

They cannot truly love hence the love

My musical king your music can never be duplicated
No matter who tries your music will never be duplicated
No one can wear your crown
Because you were specifically chosen by God
Taught by God

Your own cannot wear your crown
Because I know that they do not know
The blessings God bestowed upon you
The scope of it all
They see a father
But not the righteousness you left behind
The true teachings of God in your music that you left behind

- *Exodus*
- *Time Will Tell*
- *Natural Mystic*
- *Chances Are*
- *Three Little Birds*
- *No Woman No Cry*
- *Redemption Song*
- *Ambush in the Night*

Only one can find the light
If he looks close - do his own thing and walk in the true light of God and not in your shadow

My musical king
Your crown will forever be safe because you walked on the road of God with your music - words

None has been ordained to replace you
None will be ordained to replace you because they must be chosen by God – The True and Living God
No one can be incarnated of you because with God there are no incarnations because God does not deal with the dead he deals with Life

You are apart of our history
You will forever live on in our hearts
Our culture
Country

Like Marcus Garvey before you
Who taught his people to think progressive
Stop being regressive
The people did not listen

Now I know you were a man of good light – the light of God
Live up all of you
Like No Woman No Cry
To you and the others Cry No More
Jamaica and your people will be fine – free someday
One day they will have to listen
Learn and walk in the true and righteous way of God

To all of you that have shown us the way
Died for us
Telling us to heed your words – the words of God
True peace and blessings and may you all Rest in true Peace.

Michelle

Bobby let the impact of your music continue to impact the world
Let your voice continue to be heard
Let your beautiful melodies continue to teach and heal – heal nations the way God intended it to be
Let generations find favor and comfort in your words – songs

As humble as you were
Dean Fraser blow
Blow your Sax
Horn for a king who is now gone
But not forgotten
Take Natural Mystic to new heights
Show the world what he meant when he said
There's a Natural Mystic blowing in the air

The spirit of the song
Lose yourself in the words of this musical king
I know you can
Come on my brother blow
Let them feel the Natural Mystic within this song
Create a new rhythm

Remember the name
Remember the Jamaican in you
Ja – God made us
Remember Ja
Everyone say it when they say Ja-maica
God has never left us
This we now know

Bob Marley was correct

When he said there is a Natural Mystic blowing in the air
Jamaica – Ja is that Natural Mystic
Come on Dean
Blow like you've never blown before
Renew the union as Rasta's take fold
And beat mystically to the Kette Drum
Blow Dean Blow
Let us hear the Natural Mystic
The Natural Mystic Bob Marley sung about
The Natural Mystic that surrounds me and you
The Natural Mystic that surrounds our perfect Isle

Michelle

STONES THROWN AT JAMAICA

Jamaica what do I do with you?
What do I do with your people?
When will they learn that they are truly hurting themselves – destroying everything God has given them?

Jamaica when will your people learn that ignorance is not the key? Ignorance is a sin – ugly – regressive

Jamaica when will your people learn they cannot continue this way – on their destructive path?

They cannot continue to act foolishly
They cannot continue to walk like the blind without a guide in the dark

Father I know if you turn from them they will have nothing left
There land will be lost
Be destroyed
But how do you help a nation
A race of people that refuse to listen
A nation of people that live by ignorance
Ignorance instilled within them by their fore fathers
Their parents
Slave masters
Ignorance instilled in them due to lack of knowledge
Lack of education

They refuse to take good council
They do things that is not right
They do things that is evil
Unlawful in thy sight

Port Royal was a lesson
Hurricane Andrew, Ivan and Gilbert
They were all lessons to learn from
But still they don't listen – they continue on sinning destroying self – mashing up the country.
As soon as all is well
They become the children of Israel and Judah
They go on whoring, killing
Doing evilus things
They become like dogs without a bone
Begging bread like a crack head begging crack
A vagabond without a home

Father the young have brandished the gun
Killing without mercy
Killing for the fun
Evil has taking over your kingdom
Evil has found a home in your land – name

Father the Tsunami is on the way
They stand in its path
And this time it will be deadlier than that of the Asian Tsunami
Many will die
Many will flee
Island in chaos
Total ruin

Father they did not head the cries of your musical messenger now they will die and hell will be their eternal home
Now the Exodus will be on for some but for others without a ticket there will be no place to run. They will die – feel harsh pain.

Father they know not the hour

The day
Nor the month
Not even the minute
As they refuse to heed your call
They refuse to learn from their many hurricanes

They refuse to learn from the past
Refuse to learn from what is happening around them
Ignorance has set in them
The spell still hovers over them
A spell they refuse to let go
As it is ingrained in them

Father I am ashamed of what's happening to this blessed nation
Ashamed of what they are doing to each other – self
Father it is the only nation that has your holy name embedded in the country but they refuse your name – pollute it – bring you shame
It is the only nation that is close to you spiritually
Now they have distorted and perverted your holy hill
Your holy tabernacle
Your holy kingdom - home

Father violence has become their pillow
As they have cast aside you to follow the ways of the unrighteous – Pagans – Babylonians
They have dined with sin
Made love in sin
Now they wallow in their pits like swine's
Eating the dung of destruction – sin

Father what are they doing to themselves?
Can't they see?

Can't they open their eyes to their follies – sins?

Father what can you do to help them?
Turn them around Father
Let them follow in your lovingkindness
Change them Father
Or at least lift the spell of destruction and darkness from over them

Father, do not let them end up like the people of old that went down with hell because they did not want to give up their sinful ways.

Father help them to stop following after false gods
Vanity
The worship of men - women
Father I know you to be the truth
Let them find you once again
Let them know the truth
Turn their hearts to you father
And let them cleave to you
Like a baby cleaving to his mother's breast

Turn back the darkness from them God
Open their eyes and let them once again become a holy nation
A nation living up to your holy name
A nation living in truth

Michelle

Look at them God
Just look at them
A nation of people without shame and scorn
A nation of people that would sell you out for corn-bread

Look at them God
Look at them
A nation of people that has sold themselves for a piece of dry bread
Fifty cents

Look at them Lord
Look at them
Begging like flies eating dung
Prostituting themselves for flesh
The dollar bill

They lay in wait
Ready to kill
If you are not careful
They will steal you out of your skin
How do they sleep at nights?
Knowing their own ills – kills
How do they even teach their children?
Knowing the life they live

Look at them God
Look at them
A nation of people that follow after tricks
Are tricked
A nation of people who base their lives upon lies
More lies
A nation of people living like flies

Michelle

Father how can a nation that has your name live so unholy?

How can a nation that says they love you rape and kill you?

How can they hold their heads up when their will is to kill just because someone gave them a loaf of bread?
A dollar bill

Have they become that worthless?

Have they become a nation without pride?

A nation that would sell themselves out at a drop of a dime

Look at the children mother and fatherless
Children without pride – values

Father overstand me
See where I am going with this
Open their eyes

Let them see the ignorance in them – around them
They disgrace self and play the pity card like flies but they are fooling no one because the world see and know the hatred in them.

Look now
They have no accredited hospitals
Their sick sit around like flies
Their children lie in wait
Waiting for a man
A woman

Their next trick
Victim

Parents do not teach of abstinence
Young girls having babies like flies
Aids ravishing the nation
Future uncertain – unclear hence they die

What do they have to call their own?

They don't even have their own Airline

Not even a formal education

Economy run down like sewer going down the drain
They've become like scavengers eating dry bones
Dead flesh
The flesh of man

The poor do not have food to eat
The rich prey off the innocent
The young looting
Shooting because they have a gun nothing to eat

Life means nothing
Churches have become their play ground
Vulgar music has become their prayer
Blessed is the man (Psalms One) no longer has a home – value

Jah can no longer withstand because Jah – Jamaica has become a wasteland
They have forgotten the meaning
The motto of your sacred land

Ja – Mai – Ca which stand for God made me

Out of Many One People
Jamaica land we LOVE

We have forget this because blood run cold in paradise

The devil has made it its own
Yes its playground

They know not the scope and significance of the flag. They cannot cherish the flag and prosperity God has given them.

We have relinquished the faith yes our flag our colour because with all that we do and stand for no one knows that the flag – the colors of the flag represent true life the true life of God

But where is the truth – true love?
A new chapter begins
Soon and very soon
Disaster will strike
It will be crying time again

Crying time on the land that I truly and infinitely love

Crying time for many
Because they did not hear the trumpet blow

They did not heed the calling of the final cry

Did not heed the teachings of the reggae king – Bob Marley
The preaching and teachings of the messenger Marcus Mosiah Garvey

Now weeping comes
Death is knocking at their door
There will be no Jamaica no more

If only they would listen
Try to turn back death
Walk before death
But death walks amongst them and soon death will betray them – take them all.

Michelle

What a disaster
God you really gave these people your name
Tell me what good can come out of them when they have all betrayed you – went back on their word
What good can come out of a nation of vipers?
A nation of looters
A nation that beg like dogs
Kills at will

Look at them
Disgusting
Do they not make you ill when you look at them?
Young people killing each other like flies
Raping old people and killing them
Raping children and murdering them
People selling each other
Murdering each other
Defiling each other

Look at them
Can't even maintain their own they have to beg the World Bank like dogs begging for a bone
They are lacking Kingly and Queenly character
Do they even know the content of a character?
Do they even know the PRIDE of the Loins they came from?
The kings and queens they once were now cannot become

Father how could you have given such evil doers your name?
They lack education
Moral standards
When you look at the internet and see that this beautiful country has become the murder capital of

the world do you not hold your head down in shame?
Disgrace

Father look at them
Do they not make you ill for perverting your name?
They can't even maintain their own
Young men sitting at the road corner
Like prostitutes waiting for someone to give them bread – a bone
A decent home while young women sell themselves for a dime just to keep their fatherless children fed.

Father how can you favor them?
They do not have any shame
How can you hold your head up and look at them when they've become worse than slaves

The young refuse to plant herbs – food upon the land

You can hardly find them planting a piece of yam
But yet they would rather walk and beg
Wallow in pig sties
Wallowing in dung while begging for bread

Father look at them
Economy they have none
They would rather leave the land
Instead of making the land help them
Do they not see the future before them?
Do they not know in a short time starvation will be upon the land?

Can't they see the sea with all its abundance will no longer provide for them?

The rivers will permanently spew blood – give blood

Can't they see the sign of the times?

Can't they see their own destruction looms is near?

If only they would turn back to you
Plant a little food
A piece of yam
A little Callaloo
Corn
Tomato

Can't they see that they need to prepare and set a little bucket and capture the rain?

Can't they see that a little goes a long way?

Why can't they preserve their heritage and learn from the past by listening to wise men such as Marcus Mosiah Garvey

God why can't they preserve all the herbs you have given them so that when starvation comes they will have plenty and you can say MY CHILDREN WELL DONE

Michelle

My Collective – The Dark Side of Me – Part One

Wow Jamaica have I ever pissed you off but you deserve this cussing because the senseless violence have gone on for too long and no one is doing anything about it. I know I will face backlash. The up evil, the things you are thinking and saying about me. God have I made myself a target. The entire island must be in an uproar wanting to ambush me, even kill me.

Did not like what I said did you?   **NO**

Did I get you angry?   **YES**

Did I get the island thinking?   **YES**

Have you marked me for death and if so WHY?

Well I am glad I got you all angry maybe now each and everyone of you will take a look at the state Jamaica is in and do something about it.

Go on look outside your door and take a good look at your beautiful island and name God has given you. Take a look at each other; take a look at your improvised nation; the state of your economy, the plague of aids, the sick, the poor, educational system, the poor condition of your hospitals and police stations and roads. Look at your children and tell me you truly love them. If you said yes then why are grown men and women using them for target practice – their sexual toys?

Like it?   **NO**

Good then I have caught your attention and by pissing you all off was my way of doing it. The poems maybe crude and excessive but something needed to be done. Someone had to try and get the island to think and see where it is headed.

The state of Jamaica is in shambles. You have people our own black people that have money. People that can help but refuse, all they do is parade uptown and downtown buying infested pussy and people are homeless, in need of bread and shelter and they cannot lift a finger to help them. Some of them are a disgrace to God and man – Jamaica. They're mean – without heart and values but yet each and every day some of you are putting them on pedestals. Unnu hungry but yet some a unnu trail behind dem like wharf dog just fi get a handout. Have some ambition and try do for yourself. You are important. If you an man or woman a boneafi fren and the friendship true to the end man an man woman an woman fi si fiyu need an help you without you trailing behind them. You were the one that is there for them but as soon as some a dem reach status yu count out. And no people I am not talking about the wukliss so called fren dem wey do fi get dem anada one – wukliss.

Jamaica is a blessed country that has the name of God embedded in it so why are you acting like an unholy nation of vipers – Satan's people. When will the killing, the murders, raping and evils that you are doing stop? Can't you all see you're hurting yourselves as well as the island on a whole? Trust me the more you kill is the more you die. Let me tell all of you this so learn and know. A massive shake up is coming soon just read Jamaica Tsunami or go on the internet to view the video because soon this will be you and it will be more than crying time for many of you.

Tell me something with all that is happening on the island how far is the country right now economically. How far are you as an individual economically as well as a collective? How many of you can afford a bread? How many of you can afford to send your child or children to school on a regular basis? At times you can't find bus fare, can't even afford to buy medicine, a decent pair of shoes. Some won't live to see the next day. Why is that? What do you represent? What does Jamaica represent? What has the land become?

Daniel is being fulfilled. The sea will no longer be able to feed you. The water in the Gulf of Mexico is now polluted. How far is that water from the Caribbean? How long before the fishes and sea creatures of the Caribbean become polluted with the toxins? For those that can plant food start planting again. Think. Just suppose by fate or fluke an oil spill was to happen in the Caribbean. A tanker drifted off course. What will happen? Better yet with hurricane season looming in the distance how long before some of the toxins in the Gulf of Mexico reach the Caribbean Sea? How will this impact life in the sea? Yes I am throwing scenarios at you but you all need to know that life is real and all that is happening on your island is not necessary.

You cannot let people pay you to kill. This is not right because another man's beef is not your own. You cannot kill because it is against the law of God. It is against the law and laws of creation and the universe which is the Ying and Yang and you all know this but yet you take life senselessly. Know that the life you take have you locked and bound for hell in the spiritual. They also have your children's lives locked and your families lives locked because the life you take affect us all hence I truly pray for goodness for my children, family, the family God has truly given me as well as future generations to come.

Your dirty deeds do only affect human life it affects the earth – the land that you live on and in. For each life you take millions more are affected because you sins affect them hence death comes in the form of disasters. There is no such thing as natural disasters this is our sins being turned back upon us because everything including the ground – dirt hath life. For you that say no. Look at the yams that you grow – the trees and water and around you then come and truly talk to me.

Remember the body dies when the spirit leaves it because it is the spirit that gives the flesh life. It is the spirit that feels pain not the flesh and like I've said this is what the spirit is trying to show you. It is trying to show you that the death of spirit or the death of the spirit is harsh and far more deadly than what you are going through so why want this for you and your family – off springs? Come on now. This is not pain compared to the pain that you are going to feel in the grave trust me infinitely on this.

Remember the dead cries and we Jamaicans know this so if we know this why do we want to die and cry. Come on now. Why should someone take a life senselessly? Why put yourself in trouble for the next man? Come on now. No if im have beef with someone let him stand up and fight his or her own battles. Why should you dirty your soul – life for him or her? What about your children and family? Are they not somebody too? Man and man will forever have beef but what I find in life and what I know in life is if you do not go in the enemy's way the enemy cannot hurt you or take your life – soul. Hence we are to live according to Psalms One (1).

Look at the island. It is littered with:

- **Killing of innocent lives**
- **Aids**
- **Rape**
- **Slavery – human trafficking**
- **Poverty**
- **Devalued dollar**
- **No jobs**
- **Unstable economy**
- **Lack of investment in the island**
- **Lack of adequate education and health care**
- **Poor to no road**
- **No bauxite**
- **No airline**
- **Economic genocide**

You are making it bad for yourselves already. Jamaica owns nothing. We can't brag and show off anymore. Shit you don't even have your own airline. The last thing that was left that was proudly Jamaican is no more. You are now like unto THE DRY BONES ELIJAH was talking about because you deceived God and sold him out. Soon you won't even have a name. Now tell me what can God be proud of? He can't be proud of you if you sold him out literally. Remember our pledge of not bringing him shame and disgrace but yet we could not honor it. Each and every day we kill, steal, beg and do all manner of sin and corruption on the land. Tell me if that isn't disgrace and shame we have brought in front of God on his land – the land of Ja – Maica?

<u>So now if we shame and disgrace God in this way and he cannot trust us to honor our word (see the pledge) then why should God honor us, stand by us or even help any of us when we can't even honor him?</u>

Take a good look at what I am trying to say and think truly think about it. When you keep killing each other, raping each other, murdering the innocent, sing songs of violence, lashing out on others that do not fit into the mold of Jamaica, stop exporting food and herbs who do you think you are hurting?

Did you say you and Jamaica as a whole?

If you did ding ding ding ding ding. Bingo you have got it. So why complain? You of yourself don't want to see Jamaica do better so stop complaining if you don't have food. Most of you don't want to plant so starve because that's what you want. I know not all can plant but I am talking about those that can.

Some of you want babies and can't afford babies so you turn trouble to the system and ball mi pickney hungry. Go find the dick that got you pregnant and let him stand the responsibility because the system did not impregnate you. The system did not say spread yu leg fi mi let mi come inne mi wi support yu. Come on now. Take the dick that you love some much to court and let him support your pickney and if im can't support yu pikney tek him baby madda to court fi child support and if baby madda can't support you tek im madda and faada to court. If dem can't support you pickney tek im granny and if im granny can't support yu pickney tek im aunt or im uncle or cousin because sey dem a im family and if im caane stan the responsibility them fi stan it fi im. They are accountable for him and his sins. No but each man is accountable for their sins in this case the family is accountable for this child because I give you my word that I will petition God for this and you know what because I have written it it is a petition and it is now law between me and God so it is in affect because this law is looking out for the well being and welfare of an innocent child. Do not complain if it cause you distress because family is family and none of us can change our bloodline. As a woman or man that is duly paying child support and looking out for your own this does not apply to you but make sure you play an active role in the upbringing – decisions of your child because this is vital to your child's future.

<u>**Ladies and young girls – pickney this is your life and future. If you are not ready to have children let no one force you to have them because it is not easy raising them (children). Just take a look at the hardships some of you are facing. It gets worse because one han caane wash as I was told and this is so true. One parent cannot raise a child. Yes**</u>

many of us are doing it but none of us look at the stress, the pain and heartache of having to have to find shelter, food, clothes, money to go to school, bus fare, taxi fare, lunch money, books, school fees. It all adds up and it does contribute harshly and negatively to our well being. You could have the most money in the world it still plays on your psyche because you are doing it alone. All I have to say is XY – mother and father not X and not Y. Yes father father and mother mother XX and not X and X it takes two. Just as how it took two to give life it takes two to raise life – a child. And for those that say mi baby faada dead his family is still alive and they should contribute to the upkeep and well being of his child that is the law of God and not man.

Oh ya fi unnu oman an man wey a cuss di oman and man dem wey caane have pickney – children an a call dem eunuch, barren, dry land and whatever no mek mi cuss out unnu wasit wasit not tan tarra it claate because sey not because sey yu have pickney mek any a unnu summady. Unnu wus dan dry lan to backside because it is these women and men that have to pick up unnu what lef meaning unnu pickney wey unnu breed and get and can't manage to feed or even give a propa home – future. They are more parents than the lots of you because dem not sell pickney, dem no tun dutty bed sheet fi man or oman, dem bless but some a unnu done because sey some unnu tun unnu pickney inna taxi fare, bus fare and plane fare. Some a unnu ride di buddy till no rev and red no lef inna unnu. Some a unnu man no want because all a unnu a quick come fi dem so ress off the women and men dem that have no children because they are truly God's own. Wey unnu no tek care of fi unnu own dem and lef them alone. Why should they take up fi unnu burden them – fi unnu caane manage dem not burden. Man naa rev dem out so climb off and go mine fi unnu own if unnu can. Some a unnu wus dan scum because sey nuff a unnu no noa who di pickney faada is so unnu gi man Jacket and tie – suit and dem like fool hafi mine wey a no fi dem.

Everything I have mentioned above stops tourist from coming to your country except for my little tirades. Artist will no longer get visa's, investors will no longer invest in the country because guess what the country has become a damned liability. So why should investors lose money off of you? Shit business is business and currently Jamaica is a bad investment when you look at it from a business prospective. I see Jamaica as a poor investment because the country cannot control its trigger happy demons that are ruining the island with its guns. I would tell tourist right now not to travel to Jamaica because the island is not safe. Too much gangs are running the island and the government is not doing anything to control and eradicate these gangs off the land – island. Lives are not valued in Jamaica hence grown ass men can brutally rape innocent 8 year olds and younger and get away with it. This is our legacy. Yes there are good people on the island but there are more bad than good because like I said the guns of the island outnumber that of the police and national defense force. Tourism is down, investments forget it, artists losing visa to perform, school system failing because parents can't afford to send children to school, nurses fuming, police force raging because what the **_ISLAND IS BROKE. YOU_**

HAVE NO MONEY. WHAT'S LEFT WILL BE STARVATION FOR MANY.

Some will escape because those who have a visa for America, Canada, England, Germany, Lebanon, and Syria, you name it will flee because they have their get out of Jamaica card and will forever have it. They can leave at anytime and trust me they will when hard times hit. So think people. Who do we pree?

I don't want to get into your politricks and never will get into your politricks but what I am saying is if you truly love Jamaica and God – Jah – The Most High God then do better.

Stop the violence and let the money flow back into the country. Money can be made in Jamaica but one man or woman cannot have it, too damned greedy. We can no longer let people tell us in order to eat you have to kill – kill your own people. Come on now. Why ruin your land – your island for someone else. When you are begging bread they are well fed. Come on now. Look into yourself and do better. Why should you have to beg for the scrapings off their table? You're not dogs you're human beings that have and has a God given right to live – Life and no one has that right to take it from you if you have not given it up – sold it to the devil – the highest bidder.

The devil gives nothing freely and whatever he gives to you in the means of easy come – fast money know that you have to pay him back with your soul – life. You infinitely will have no part in

God's abode because you gave up your life to the devil's own.

No one has a right to take your life or even hold you hostage for it. It is wrong. God does not do it so why should man and the evil – wicked and evil people do it? Come on now. Right is right and fair is fair. What makes your life more important than mine? No come on now. What makes your life more important than mine? And material possessions don't make you better than me because we all die the same way meaning death takes us and we are buried or burned the same way meaning our dead bodies go under the earth. No I should recant that because good life is priceless and worth more than diamonds and pearls – white gold not yellow gold because when evil is burning and stinking up the place good people will be at peace true peace and rest with God – the True and Living God so in this case good people are better than you. We have God and you got evil and his pay and woe be unto you when the death angel takes you.

Young kids start planting – do something. Yes it takes time but you know what nothing was built overnight. Also remember easy come easy goes.

Artist stop the negativity because those that you lash out against run the world. They sit in every major organization around the globe. God said true love not hate. Think. You are the ones crying now and you have a right to cry because God does not tolerate hatred and it is not right. So who is crying now? Remember family need to be fed, bills need to be paid so how are you going to pay it and still drive your fancy car and live in your elaborate mansions if there is no money coming in?

Politicians I have to come here because I hate politics and hope God forgives me for meddling in your affairs but you as individuals and as a collective can and must do better for the future of Jamaica.. Instead of raping the country and running it bankrupt *help your people and the island.* Fix up the island and stop raping – stealing the country of its wealth and prosperity because the money that comes into the country does not belong to you it belongs to Jamaica. From you take a penny that does not belong to you you are a fucking thief and that make your family and pickney a fucking thief. Many of you are thieves because you leave the island and parishes that you represent impoverished and broke and woe be unto the lot of you because what you steal you must repay even in death.

Come on, I want to see Jamaica up there when it comes to trade. Instead of being stigmatized as a third world country why not strive to be a developed nation. The island has every resource at its finger tips why not encourage the youths to get a quality education, improve your hospitals, police force and **FIX YOUR DAMNED ROADS**. They are damned deplorable a disgrace. It's like driving in hell down there. Come on you want to attract tourist fix your damned country. Maybe then tourist will come back and spend more of their hard earned money.

Young girls some of you are nastier than sin. Take some damned pride in yourself and have some damn ambition for yourself because none of you are clean just smell unnu draws krachies. Some a it no original coula no lef inna it. Di krachies yellow. Some a unnu rev out like taxi cab. Grow up and have ambition and stop mek man use unnu like golf course. No not golf course because golf course are for the elite. It's the elite tool but inna fi unnu case race course – the one wey horse run pan. Ambition goes a long way and from one talk all talk and sey yu a easy ride – trick.

Some a unnu madda wukliss because dem si an noa an uphold the slackness. Some a dem fi hog tie and beat. Teach your children good values so that they can grow up and teach their children good values also.

Look how many young girls down there (in Jamaica) that are battling AIDS and HIV come on now. Men are so nasty because some know women have HIV and AIDS but yet sleep with them unprotected. Was is necessary to give these girls your incurable germs? How many of you have your wives that are battling AIDS because you can't keep your dick in your pants?

Girls if you are going to have sex with anyone make sure that they are clean and use protection because it is vital to your survival. It is not right for anyone to come and take away your life. 2-5 minutes of pleasure is not worth it so weight the cost. It is your life so do not give it away foolishly. If you can abstain abstain because in truth men are not worth the trouble when it comes to life. They are not worth the stress because some did not grow up with good values. Know the good ones from the bad ones and infinitely stay away from the bad ones because the life you save will be your own.

Whether you like it or not here are some of my suggestions to catapult Jamaica into the future:

Government talk to your people about the violence and do all that you can to try to curb it. Tell them they are hurting the island and themselves because they are. When tourists do not come to Jamaica how will the bills be paid? Teachers, doctors, lawyers, police officers, government officials, the country's debt to the IMF how will these bills be paid? Make the people see. Your roads are in utter disrepair. Take a drive in Clarendon and St. Catherine. Some of the roads are filled with craters and nothing is being done about it. Come on which tourist want to see that. I most certainly don't. People look down on you come on now.

Try to encourage tourist to come to island again by ensuring their safety.

Give the youths incentives and invest in youth programs. You have world class runners. What about a world class soccer team, encouraging kids to play basketball, tennis, and baseball? You never know when one will be drafted and more.

Export more yams, banana, ginger, guava, jackfruit, mangoes, lime leaf, june plum, breadfruit, sweet potatoes, peas, beans, pears you name it try to get the country on board with Canada, The United States, Africa, the world. When I go to the grocery I am tired of not seeing the Jamaican name on the shelf. Reason, I want to see Jamaican Avocado (pear) but when I look closer the pears come from another country. Come on that is insulting and disrespectful. Companies a use the Jamaican name to sell their crap and the sugar and flour don't even come from Jamaica. Why should someone else exploit the Jamaican name and Jamaica is not benefitting from it? Come on now. This is f---ry on the highest level come on now. Don't use the Jamaican name to sell your garbage because the product does not come from Jamaica and it is high time we as Jamaican's stop buying these bogus products. They're not benefitting the country so why buy them – support them come on now. We complain that Jamaica is broke but yet we do not support our own. What sense does that make? Are we that ignorant and daft?

We know the food is good and is organic, not chemically produced why not do more for the farmers that cultivate these products? Right now China – Taiwan control the market for exports why not get on the bandwagon with them and lead Jamaica forward in a positive and good way.

Those that can afford to have bed and breakfast lodges for visitors who just want to stay a night or two do so. But make sure the place is clean, safe, comfortable and affordable. Some of us need those two days away from family to unwind and have some fun. The more intimate the setting the better. Meaning an area for dinner and dancing would be nice.

How about having a restaurant within the airport lounge where people that have long flights can get something to each before taking the plane. Lots of people are diabetic and need to eat in order for their blood sugar not to dip. **Don't even go there with the** *negative thinking. When you do that then Jamaica will be back to square one. Tourist will stop come and Jamaica will be labeled with becoming a drug trafficking country. We are trying to uplift Jamaica not bring it down people so forget those thoughts. You don't need it.*

Young kids have your little stall maybe by the seashore along the airport strip and sell your little corn, jerk chicken, jerk whatever, coconut water whatever. Just do something for you to generate an income to help you through school.

Jamaica have many working class people that don't have breakfast in the mornings why not have a breakfast house or coffee house that sell coffee, tea, bagels, muffins. Even sell stuffed patties. No Mr. Patty companies you cannot make stuffed patties because a stuffed patty is made to order by the client – customer and for you to do it would be unhealthy. A stuffed patty can consist of lettuce. Or it can consist of a slice of cheese with mayonnaise and lettuce. It is served hot not cold. All the staff have to do is open the patty and place these extras in it. So you can have that as a part of your breakfast menu.

For those who want to take it further how about having lunch trucks or lunch carts and cater to the office worker if there are no cafeterias in the building that they work for.

Make sandwiches, roast breadfruit and sell it with ache and salt fish or chicken. Sell hot dogs – wieners on a bun. Do you see where I am going with this? And please don't go set up shop so get permission from the place of business first. You cannot violate their privacy just like that.

What about having a French Fry company that sells seasoned curly fries or just plain fries throughout the Caribbean?

People some of you can make potato salad and sell it on a daily basis and once again hygiene. Your place must be clean and sanitary.

There is Macaroni Salad and Cole Slaw that you can make and sell to generate income. You can sell to the coffee trucks and restaurants. The restaurants can use your product as a side dish on their menu. And yes I will state hygiene and sanitation because they are critical. You have to think about people's health and health concerns. So make sure your station or place is sanitary.

For the nail salons do pedicures to get some of the crust off the bottom of our feet. Have you seen some of the crusty foot dem lately? No for real have pedicure and be clean. Need I remind you of hygiene hygiene hygiene? I cannot stress this anymore because hygiene is vital.

How about having all you can eat buffets? No scrap that because some of us will come with more than our bellies.

If there are no flea markets around how about having flea markets that are open on Saturdays and Sundays only.
How about having bingo halls for seniors to come and play and win some money. I know ordinary

people will come but hey that's okay as long as they are not rowdy.

Kids you have a color printer at home. Some of you have black and white but expand and do birthday flyers, baptism flyers for people who are having birthdays and christenings. Be innovative with the tools you have and make it work for you in a positive and good way. Some of you are geniuses when it comes to making videos and posting them on you tube. Charge a small fee and catalog your work. Listen you don't need a big and elaborate production this I know so capitalize on the market while you still can.
If food is not your thing how about selling flowers a rose or two or three.

Make suck suck and sell it out of your homes.

Write beautiful poetry put them in frames and sell them.

And people don't rob or steal from them. Encourage these kids because they are doing something for themselves, something of benefit. Parents help and encourage your kids if this is what they want to do. They are doing something and not picking up the gun.

Those that can make straw hats, why not do it. Make bags-purses that are elegant and beautiful so that when tourists see it they want to buy it. Be reasonable with pricing and don't price them too high that we can't afford to buy your product.

Artist if you can draw sorry it's not if you can draw because you can. Why not charge ten or twenty US to draw pictures of tourist, same in Canadian funds?

Government why not try to sell Jamaican Weed. Yes I went there to the pharmaceutical companies globally. We know it's good for pain why not capitalize on it. Shit India and Pakistan cultivate Heroin for commercial use in pharmaceuticals why not Jamaica with its Ganja. Why destroy what God has given you. Use it to benefit the country economically. There are many people that are sick across the globe if this plant helps them why not help these people.

UWI I would like to see renewable energy come out of your campus. What's happening with you? Come students give the developed nations a run for there money. I challenge the lot of you to develop renewable energy and bring Jamaica into the future. Take solar energy and wind energy to a whole new level. Come on devise ways to conserve energy. I've heard Jamaican can do anything step up and show the world Jamaica has balls. Remember the Jamaican Bobsled team. If you can have a bobsled team in a hot climate you most definitely can lead the way when it comes to renewable energy.

Also UWI students try to develop an energy efficient nozzle that fit on water tanks; a nozzle that filters and kills bacteria – make **_RAIN WATER_** fit for human consumption for years or lengthy periods of time. The reason I am telling you to do this is because **_WATER WILL BECOME A COMODITY ON THE STOCK MARKET_**

GLOBALLY. WATER WILL BE VALUED MORE THAN GOLD AND PLATINUM COMBINED and this is due to the water shortage to come globally. Many people will die because they won't be able to afford drinking water and those that cannot afford it will loot and yes die. Many will die because of the high global price. Yes the rich man will die too because soon he will not be able to afford it. So please do not let greed cause you to become greedy. Do not put greed first because if you do you too will die.

Food will become a high valued commodity also so farmers start farming because food is needed and yes soon people will not afford to buy it because all will be spent on getting a little water. We need water for everything so farmers secure your land and start building tanks on your land, underground tanks that go above ground and fill the up with rain water. Each time the rain fall let your catch basin from your roof fill it up. Do not waste the rain water because soon you will truly need it.

For all you people that have pit toilets by the river stop this practice and move your pit toilet away from the river banks because river water is need and soon you will need it to drink so stop polluting the water.

I know what some of you are saying but trust me God cannot come into a dirty planet that is riddle with sin – filth. What he does he send his messengers – people that have some semblance of truth – and (when I say this it is because we too have sinned) to guide you on the right path. God cannot come out of the sky and save you, you have to save yourself. And for those that are going to run to your pastors and listen to them tell you not to listen to me you will go down with sin – die because when pastor have and have to ration he won't be thinking of you and God will not spare you because you did not listen – you listened to man. So secure your own from now and listen. Right now God is trying to save you from what is to come so listen.

Man will start eating man and trust me the murders and Don's of the land will be no exception because man will not be able to afford food so they have to resort to eating self – humans to keep them alive. Trust me the menu will read serving humans only because we cannot find meat to eat. This is not a Sci-Fi movie. Soon this will be reality because we made it so. We destroyed the resources of the planet hence the destruction of this world comes before 2032. We gave up 2132. So the extinction of man comes – death comes due to our sins. Yes we can change this hence I tell good people do not worry about sin and all sins doing because sin must get paid and their payment is death. The flesh of the wicked must be eaten by the scorpion kings hence man will cry – suffer.

Good people I've told you, you are whom God is concerned about. He is not concerned about wicked and evil people because sin has them – they made a pact with the devil and in all that they do they do not see that they are bound by the devil – sin and because of this – they giving their lives to death – sin they must die a harsh death with sin. I've told you when you give your wealth, money, time and effort to sin you will die with sin hence we God's people – children can no longer buy the goods of sin. We can no longer dance with sin, sing with sin, marry sin, die in sin, do business with sin, or have children with sin. When we continue to do this we become like sin and we too must die. We are giving away God's blessings when we do this and this is a slap in the face of God – the True and Living God. You have to know what you're doing because Noah's Ark is now. And no God will infinitely never ever allow sinful and wicked demons – people in his ark so scrap the shit the bible told you about unclean animals. That is bullshit. Sin is seeking importance with man because sin knows he hath none – no importance in LIFE or with God.

Never, infinitely never forget in all that sin does he seeks to destroy good – life hence the world is in a shambles today. Sin hath no life – truth so sin must lie in order to take your life and destroy you in the end.

Good people – the children of God know that God does not kill his people and it is sin – wicked and evil people that must die and this is why you must now separate yourself from them. LIVE BY PSALMS ONE AND LIVE. Prepare for that which is to come and live right and you will be spared the death of sin. I AM TELLING YOU THIS BECAUSE IT WAS TOLD TO ME "WALK BEFORE DEATH" meaning keep out the pathway of death and live. Live for Life – God and you will be okay but you must be true to life – God meaning you must be honest. So prepare because soon many will have no water or food to eat. God is warning you because when the famine comes and you have no food to eat or drinking water you cannot blame

God you can only blame you because you were duly warned.

Trust me all the money that man save up for self will be for naught because the one that has the water will be the richest man alive – he will have the key to life and death. Silver and gold will mean nothing in the end, pharmaceutical will become a thing of the past because all the diseases that man has created to kill man people will seek them to die a quick death so that they won't be cooked or eaten alive literally.

Gas – oil will become a thing of the past because soon there will be none. Yes the oil wells went dry.

House – mortgaged house will be abandoned and banks will go broke because there will be no jobs around to pay for them – pay the banks back. Everything will be lost expect for those that own their own. Everyone will cry pity the poor – a little water to spare my life but he will get none because goodness will be gone from man. He the poor man will die because he too did not listen.

<u>We forgot we gave death the key – an all access pass to lie – kill.</u>

<u>Know – infinitely know that God will never save the dead because God is life and he does not deal with the dead nor the living dead.</u>

Still pissed off at me?   ***YES***

Sorry but people you need to think and use your head. We need money to flow back on the island.

The poor need to eat food and kids need to go to school.

Maybe I am over my head and have stupid suggestions but it doesn't hurt to expand your horizon. I know Jamaica export yam and sweet potatoes to Canada but what about expanding your market globally. If you can't sell tourists on the health benefits of organic coconut water that it has potassium and it is good for the heart. Guava is good for the heart and well as it aids in helping you to lose weight and lower blood pressure. Ginger helps to reduce blood pressure. Watermelon is good for the body. Also, if you can't get the market encourage tourist to take some of these fruits back home with them and ensure it is legal for them to bring it back to their country. Come on if you can't get to the mountain let the mountain come to you.

See where I a going with this.

I don't want to buy Jamaican Flags made in India or China when I come to Jamaica. I want to buy Jamaican flags made by Jamaican's. Yes it's cheaper to make and I have nothing against these nations but why not try to compete. Get some of the global market by attracting investors that is willing to invest in the country. Instead of having Jamaican coffee in Starbucks alone what about having Jamaican coffee in Tim Horton's? Trust me they have a hell of a lot more stores than Starbucks and Coffee Time combined. How about selling Jamaican coffee in the grocery stores all across Canada, the United States and the world? Cause you know Jamaican coffee is great – the best better than all the rest. Yes people I am being biased but I have to sell sell sell and this is the only way I know to do it. So when in Jamaica have a cup of real Jamaican Java and compare it to the rest and then tell me. Don't be brutal though be kind and gentle because you all know my mouth hence you are duly warned.

Jamaican's have I got your attention. You need these things. This is the twenty first century and your nation is impoverished. If Jamaica continue on its course what will happen to your children and grand children? What good legacy will they have if any? You as a collective of people, you as an individual, the government must be held accountable for the future of your children and grand children. When you continue to screw up the country what will they inherit? Do you want them to inherit an impoverished country or do you want them to be proud and hold their heads up high.

There is a multitude of wealth across the globe and Jamaica has the resources to achieve greatness but you need to want it and see what Marcus Garvey was preaching. Instead of people a nation of regressive people, be progressive come on now. **_Right now Jamaica has a regressive mentality but remember out of straw you can get gold. Money people._**

So if each and every individual truly love Jamaica live up to your name the name and land that God has given you. God never forgot about Jamaica. Jamaica forgot about God. Remember, Bob Marley said no matter how much they kill the saints of God many more will come.

Take warning if you as a nation don't wake up and heed the calling as well as the name of God you will not like the consequences because God will for a surety leave you all to your doom and corruption. He will take his name and land from you.

Rasta's you are not without fault. You know the name of God. You know that which is correct but yet you are not doing anything to benefit the country. It's good to sing about true love, preach about love but it is greater when you do out of true love. Sing about truth not lies. Band together and help your country as a unit and stop letting the devil infiltrate your holy hill. You are Jah – maicans. Jamaica is whom you should give props to. Right now Jamaica is like unto Babylon with its iniquity and evils. Pluck the beams out of Jamaica's eyes before you pick it out of others because each and everyday bodies lay waste on the island. Represent your own which is Jamaica. That is why God gave you a land of your own and all of you see and turn a blind eye to it.

How many of you have stepped up to the plate to help Jamaica and its people in a positive way? But yet you ride off the coat tails of Jamaica preaching about loving Jah – please you're all infestation of locust prying off Jamaican bread. None of you truly love Jamaica because all of you walk in the pagan way and do as the pagans do. You talk the pagan way and dress like the pagans therefore you all represent the pagans – the pagan way. When you sit back and do nothing to help your own you are like a Pagan – a Babylonian because you acknowledge what they do. So therefore you are not holy but sinful because you have not charity – truth. Don't even come to me with the Rasta colors or the colors of Jamaica because I know what the colors represent and none of you can represent it hence you represent Ethiopia and can't, indefinitely can't represent your own – Ja – Mai – Ca. You represent death – the land of the Ethers – gaseous people. You cannot represent Life – Ja-Mai-ca. You have all turned your backs on Jamaica hence you're all backwards. You turned against God for the devil's own so continue to represent them. Better yet why the hell doesn't the lot of you go live with them? You want to represent nasty so go be with nasty because they too sold out God by trampling on his holy ground. They sold God out long ago hence many of them are mixed breed – bred with the devil's own. And not because the bible has them in it because the bible is the devils own – the book of sin and deceit. Why do you think they have Ethiopia in the Bible? They know what they did so they had to be included but as always we do not listen to God nor do proper research. We just accept any shit people give us and say "YES A DI TRUTH. DI BIBLE IS HOLY AND FROM GOD" but yet within this holiness it is filled with shit – deceit. All manner of evil you can find in this book. People use it fi obeah, witchcraft, voodoo and unnu say it is of God. What is so different between it and the book of Macabes? Are they both not unholy? And none a unnu no ask mi bout di Macabes because I have never seen one or read one. And infinitely no I do not want one because God is educating me and not you.

You all should be ashamed for representing another man's land that isn't even your ancestral home. Tell me what did God do to you for you to do this to him?

Don't use the name Jah, use the name Eth because that's who you pose up and represent. I hope in the end the Ether's can represent you – save you because I know they don't respect you.

Don't pose up the triangle if you can't represent it right. Don't pose off on it if you can't maintain it because the triangle isn't given unto the unrighteous. I am not saying you are unrighteous but the triangle when put together represents the Star of David. The key to unity. The union of man and the divine for those of a higher order.

The triangle is a seal. A key and it is not any and anybody can use the seal so you had better be clean to walk under the order of the triangle. I am not saying anymore because you know the truth as well as know the knowledge of the higher plains.

So to all yes I have pissed you all off but now I have you thinking. If you have read this passage and your eyes are not open to the future and the greatness you as an individual can do as well as a nation then you're truly lost and don't deserve to be saved.

Yes you can hate me all you want but the truth is Out of Many One People. Each and every one of you is under one banner which is the Jamaican banner. No other nation is like unto you so you had better start changing and hold your head up high or Jamaica will have nothing and none of you will have anyone to blame but you yourself. Each individual can make a difference. Do not look at the great picture. Look at the small picture and expand on it. Remember a baby doesn't just get up and walk he or she must be taught to sit up, then creep, then hold on, then to walk.

Yes I am tired of us disrespecting self and blaming it on others when we are to blame also. Hence I say do your homework and stop harping on slavery because if you did your research you would know that the black race sold our own people long before the white man started doing it. We sold our own to the white man so you have to blame self – our ancestors for this also. You cannot just blame one race of people. Go back in history to the Babylonians. Did we not sell our people to them as slaves to clean their homes? Are black people still not in the land of Nod today? They were the little people of our ancestry and they live amongst the dead so be fair. Like I said you cannot teach lies and expect your children to come and know the truth they will only know lies and continue your tradition of teaching lies and growing in lies. We the black race is guilty of sin because we became sinful because Eve was not white she was black and Adam was Indian not black because he was from the land of Nod. He was not a good person hence Adam is the first devil – Satan. Know that God did not forbid Eve from marrying him because of sin tone. He forbade her from marrying or getting involved with him because he was evil – pure and utter evil. Know, infinitely know the truth. The children of the South were forbidden to marry or get involved with the people of the North because they practiced sin – evil and good and evil should have never mingled. She broke the circle of truth and introduced evil onto the land and this is why evil is on the four corners of the globe. Hence you have the four rivers, the four lands. Yes the cross of death that your church has you believing in because the cross represents the time line evil got on this land to deceive and mislead. The church will not invert the cross they must keep it upright to keep deceiving you. They know if the invert the cross you would know that all they do is evil. True evil must invert the cross. It is a must because evil goes down and never up. Evil cannot go up to God – Life it can only go down in death – to death.

Know that not all blacks in Egypt were born there. They came from other lands and culture also. We were the ones to give the Babylonians the key to invade and dominate our land. We gave them the key to pollute the earth and that started with Eve. She did this. We did this so we are all guilty of sin. Good life did not come from Eve evil life did hence the devil will forever try to infiltrate and duplicate the triangle but can never do this because the triangle is not given to evil it is given to good – LIFE.

We the black race caused the rift and instead of fixing it we play the blame game and let the rift continue to spread – widen. We accept crap that other people feed us by saying it is the truth. We are the ones to forget our history. We are the ones to soil it. We are the ones to give up life for death. We are the ones to want what the next man has and if we can't get it or don't get it we kill him or her for it.

What God has given you is yours not the next man but yet we sell it out – don't want the land and gifts he has given us. We are to keep what God has given up so why sell it out then halla and ball in the end? Does that make any sense?

Jamaica owns nothing but yet we cry. God did not sell out Jamaica Jamaicans did so don't cry to God if you gave up your own.

We do not want the name of God.
We do not want his land.
We do not want to have anything to do with God hence we go into churches deemed to be for God dirty and unclean. We wear our shoes in church disrespecting God so why should God respect you or even listen to you when each and every day we disrespect him.

Unnu neva think about God so why the hell should God have mercy on any of you. No don't cry out for mercy or salvation because none of us show God mercy or salvation.

God cannot take back what you have sold infinitely know this. Once it's gone it's gone. You sold it God had nothing to do with it. You never thought about your future or your children's future so suffer. Many of you want it all hence we let greed dictate our lives. The greedy man sees himself and cannot see others hence he do thing to take it all – control and dominate thinking he has ultimate power. But what is power when you hath not Life – God?

Many of you without jobs who's to blame? You let the violence escalate. You give the murders and rapists free reign over the land. They have all the rights because they are not being held accountable.

Do not cry anymore because we allow this to happen. Not one of you have sought help from the international community to put pressure on your government to clean up the island of the senseless violence and raping of our children. You guys like the violence hence nuff a unnu are being fed and clothed by your Don man and yes Don oman.

Have any of you ever given thought to life. Grown ass men and women are raping our children this is wrong. Babies come on man – these children are babies and men and women are raping them and the island condone this. Just sit back like it is not going to affect them. Musicians know people – politicians know people – lawyers know people – Don man and oman know people but instead of being the voice of the innocent and cry out to the international community for help they keep their damned mouths shut and condone this practice. Some a unnu especially unnu Don man if it was your child this was happening to blood woulda run like riva in a Jamaica until your blood was cooled and thirst quenched. None of you ever thought that we were responsible for each other no matter color or creed. Every human being on the face of this planet is responsible for each other's child. We are accountable for them because they are children and it is our responsibility to teach them right and not wrong. They are not sex toys for adults – they are children and we as parents are their true voice until they get older.

We say the children are our future so if we screw them up from now meaning when they are young how can they become our future or have a future?

Will they not do wrong?

Will they not become even more screwed up than us?

Will they not become more vile than us?

Remember God did not make us slaves nor did he make us closed mouth. No one has a right to muzzle you for the truth because we are not dogs we are humans. So di shut mouth sinting do not work. You cannot bask in the offerings of the devil and not expect to get paid one day. No hear and deaf see and blind sinting does not work when it comes to our children. We cannot be held hostage and the government and police force cannot hold a NATION hostage if you come together in unity for a positive and good goal.

Right now the government is trying but how many of you are dying senselessly with the no foul language act. This is a breach of your fundamental rights. A breach of your freedom of speech but yet you sit and absorb it instead of taking the Government of Jamaica for violating your fundamental rights – Freedom of Speech.

Remember the government need you, you don't need them. They need your votes at election time and you can demand a early election if they are not governing right. Come on now.

Without your money the police force and government workers will not get paid. You have them by the balls because if everyone stand up and say I am not paying your taxes until you fix the road, the schools, the hospitals, police stations, the violence and crime that is plaguing the island they cannot do a damned thing about it.

The government is responsible for the infrastructure of Jamaica. Meaning it is their job to fix the road, fix the crime that is plaguing the island, fix the schools and provide adequate living conditions for its people. Some of you should not be living if filth – shit literally. The government is not doing its job so take the government to court. The international courts and let them be charge with neglect – neglecting your fundamental human and God given rights. Take the government to court. What do you have a court system for? Let the courts do their damned job because as it is right now every Jamaican can take the Jamaican government to court for breach of contract.

If your boss or co-worker is harassing you and you can prove it do you not take them to court for damages?

If your baby daddy is neglecting your child do you not take him to court?

What makes the government any different?
Is the government not failing you as a citizen?
Is the government not failing the country on a whole?
Are your constitutional rights not being violated? Come on now. Stop settling and so something for you. The infrastructure of the island meaning roads, building, hospitals, schools, government run homes, are the responsibility of your government and they are neglecting them and you so sue their ass. If you

repair something for them because you cannot stand it send the government a bill of repair and I would not advise anyone to repair what is the government's responsibility. They the government get the money so hold them accountable. They money belongs to Jamaica not the elected officials. You cannot have them bankrupting the country and raping it of its wealth come on now.

Trust me none of you want me to run Jamaica because my first order of business would be to fire everyone in cabinet and in the senate. Trust me all dem lawyers wey a sit pan bench and collect free cheque their ass would be fired quicker than you can say Jesus wept. If you cannot respect the island and its people then none of you should be in office.

And trust me every Prime Minister dead or alive would be sent a bill – billed in equivalent to the countries national debt. Every cabinet member no matter the party will get a bill and they would have to repay it hence their expensive cars, land and homes will be confiscated and sold. Swiss bank accounts will have to be turned over to the government because the money rightfully belongs to the government. Yes businesses too. And it's the family of the dead Prime Ministers that would have to pay back the debt and the same rule applies to them for the prime ministers that are living. No one would be immune. Corrupt officers, doctors the same rule applies. If they can't pay then their family must pay because they did raise them wrong – to steal. Like I said we are the ones to teach wrong so in doing so we have to pay.

Salaries gotten over the years will infinitely have to pay back because they did not do anything positive for Jamaica they just ruined it – the land and its people. Why should they get paid for sitting on their fat and skinny lazy asses and dictate to people when they are so backwards – inept. Educated fools except for one because in no let me shut mi mouth deyso because this will be all out war and true me peaceful duppy noa who fi frighten and lie to and it's so not me hence mi a go kibba mi tongue until due time. But for real you cannot let the educated inept dictate to you or run the country because none have the best interest of Jamaica and Jamaicans at heart. None can deny this because all I have to do is point to the 18.2 billion Us and rising National Debt Load.

For all you rapist – men and women that use children as sex toys. Trust me I would have a deal with the Russian Government. Reason being the coldest place on earth is in Russia hence I would have a deal with them for you rapist scum bags that use people's children as sex toys. I would ensure you all have a place there to stay and as soon as you get off the bus, train or plane or even car your dick is widely exposed to the elements. Trust me your dick – penis will freeze in less than thirty second and all the officials has to do is box it off – slap it off. When you are thawed out you would be in so much pain. No medical attention would be given to you and you can consider this JUSTICE BEING SERVED for the innocent life you've fucked up and taken for a lifetime. Trust me God will not punish these officials because God knows how I feel about degenerate scumbags – cesspools of the worst kind of shit that walks the face of the planet earth like you. Trust me those words are mild to the comparison of you. Trust me death knows to make the spiritual fire infinitely hotter for scumbags like you. No mercy will be given because the more you cry out for mercy is the more the fire gets hotter. This is my vengeance on the wickedest – darkest scale.

What right do you have to do this – hurt innocent children?

No it burns me so deep that God knows the way I infinitely feel.

What mother fucking right do you have to rape children of their innocence – dignity? And you the government are worthless for giving them a place in jail and providing food for scumbags like these. Trust me I would give them no bed to sleep on, no soap to bathe; no food to eat. If they want food you would have to use your fingers and till the ground or let your family feed you because trust me I would bake the shit of children and give you to eat for food. Murders trust me you wouldn't even get legal aid – government lawyers to represent you. You took a life so why should the government give you rights. You will have none. You too would get the same treatment as the rapist – pedophile.

No I would give you water to drink and soap to bathe because disgust hath nothing on you, you didn't rape an innocent child. But your punishment will be harsh none the same you would have to work to eat and infinitely you would have to support the family financially for the life you have taken. If you cannot do it then your family have to do it. You will owe that family for life. Anything that family needed you would have to do because you did take an innocent life and for this you have to pay and pay dearly. So if that family requires you to be their slave for life then a slave you must be. If they beat you every day for laziness or for just beat for nothing at all it is their right because you did take an innocent life. Any medical expenses that the family incur you have to pay them because you did take an innocent life. Yes I know accidents happen – car accidents where death occur and you are liable hence you have car insurance and the payout for the accident must go to the family of the life or lives you have taken. They is no way around this. Yes this rule can be amended but with all information given and both families – parties coming together with a viable agreement – solution.

No cheating or cohering is allowed because if it is both parties will be in default and neither of you will get anything. All MONIES will go to charity or a struggling family or hospital.

And yes it will be a criminal offence not to be charitable. Meaning you will be charged and held liable for not giving to the poor and needy.

Hence the DARKSIDE OF ME and now you know the truth of "AND LOW MAN HAS BECOME LIKE ONE OF US KNOWING GOOD AND EVIL"

You also know the truth of Judges **_hence the wicked must die and pay for their evils. This we leave to death hence I will tell you work no evil and do no evil. Leave wicked and evil people alone and let_**

death handle them in true time which is the time of God – that which was allotted to evil.

Good knoweth evil hence we have Will. For the good it's not about death nor is it about revenge it's about punishment – justice – true justice being served.

No we cannot play God or be God hence vengeance is left to death and not God. Know the law and laws of men is not of God – they are of men and men only because as humans we do not know what God's laws are. If we did I would not be writing this book and the people of this world would be good law abiding citizens. We would respect each other and each other's own.

So people please do not put my name on any ballot box if you know what is good for you. You are duly warned and I've asked you kindly and in truth. I love Jamaica infinitely and truly love hence I get on your cases and piss you all off for you to do better. I need you all to respect the land and name God has given you because like I said if you can't respect yourself you cannot respect God – Ja – Mai – Ca.

Michelle

Other books by Michelle Jean:

My Collective the Other Side of Me

Behind the Scars

My Collective A Collection of Prayers Sayings and Poems

Coming soon:

A Little Journey